BLACKHAWKS PUBLISHING
1901 West Madison Street
Chicago, IL 60612

John F. McDonough, President & CEO
Jay Blunk, Executive Vice President
Adam Kempenaar, Senior Director, New Media and Creative Services
John Sandberg, Creative Director
Sean Grady, Graphic Designer, Creative Services
Bob Verdi, Blackhawks Historian
Chase Agnello-Dean, Manager, Photography
Emerald Gao, Coordinator, New Media and Creative Services
Leah Hendrickson, Coordinator, Social Media
Eric Lear, Reporter, New Media
Leah Pascarella, Intern, New Media
Tessa Hursh, Intern, Photography and New Media

ONE GOAL III: THE INSIDE STORY OF THE
2015 STANLEY CUP® CHAMPION CHICAGO BLACKHAWKS

EDITOR
Adam Kempenaar

CREATIVE DIRECTOR
John Sandberg

ASSOCIATE EDITOR
Emerald Gao

FEATURE WRITER
Bob Verdi

CONTRIBUTORS/EDITORIAL ASSISTANCE
Eric Lear
Leah Hendrickson
Leah Pascarella
Tessa Hursh

COVER DESIGN/ILLUSTRATIONS
Sean Grady

PHOTOGRAPHY
Chase Agnello-Dean
Bill Smith
Rudi Ayasse
Kena Krutsinger
Steve Woltmann
Amber Fry
Tessa Hursh
Getty Images
Hockey Hall of Fame

ADDITIONAL COPYEDITING
Glynis Gibson

PRINT COORDINATION
Jamie Carter
Rock Communications
1117 East 14th St. North
Newton, IA 50208

PRINT PRODUCTION
Color FX
10776 Aurora Ave.
Des Moines, IA 50322
colorfxprint.com

THE INSIDE STORY OF THE 2015 STANLEY CUP® CHAMPION CHICAGO BLACKHAWKS

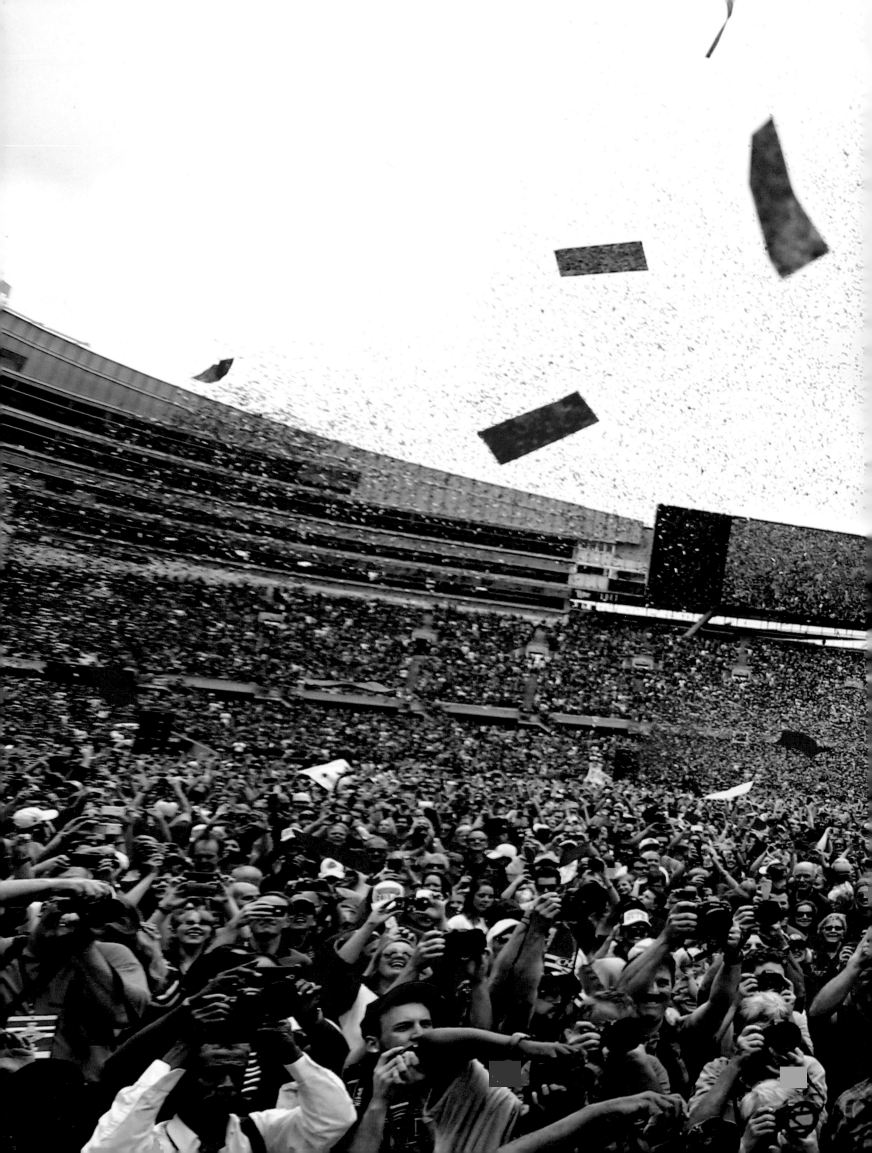

TABLE OF CONTENTS

INTRODUCTION

THE BLACKHAWKS WAY   I

CHASING HISTORY   II

DREAMING IN COLOR III

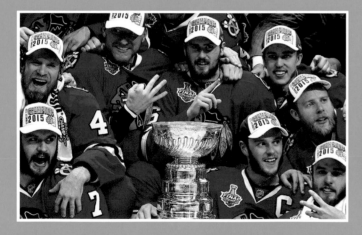

WINNING AT HOME IV

CELEBRATING STANLEY V

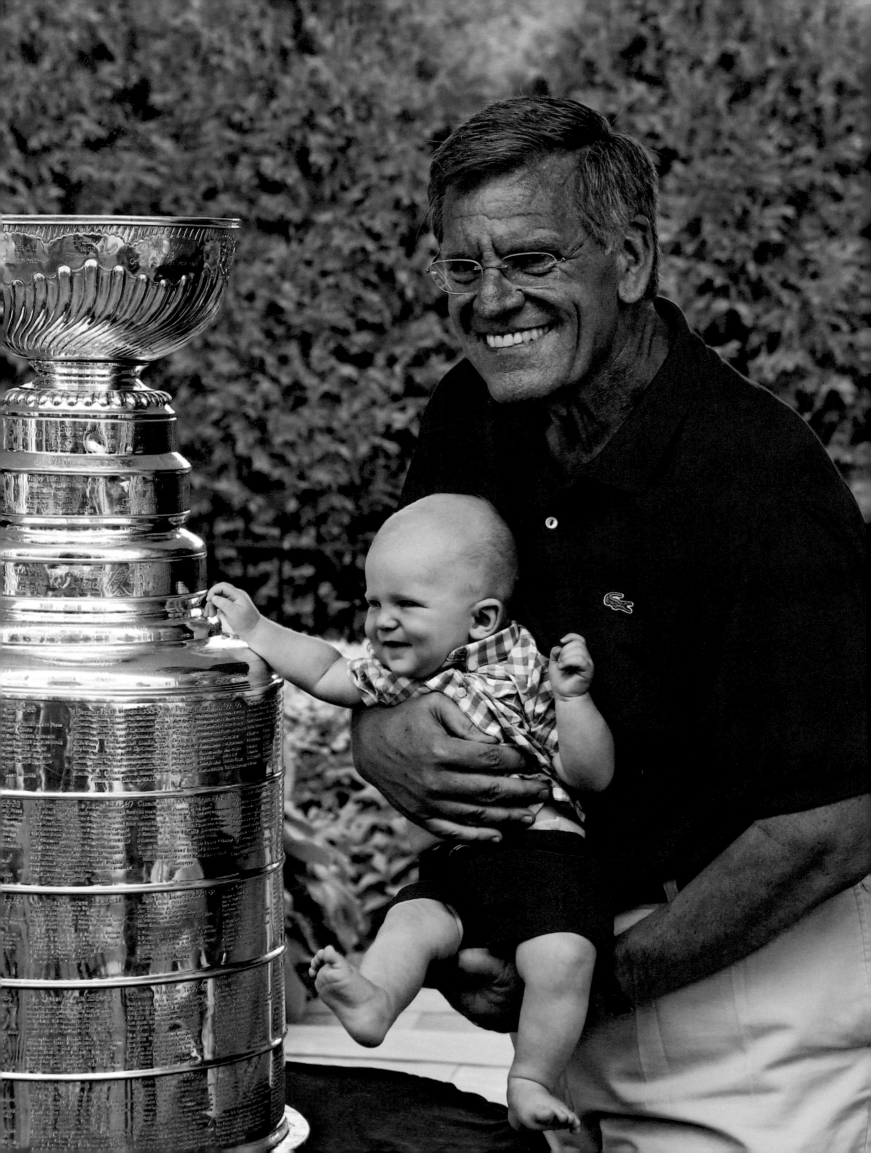

NEVER TURNING BACK

by W. ROCKWELL WIRTZ, CHAIRMAN

The Blackhawks' performance down the stretch of the 2015 playoffs reminded me of a racehorse. When a good horse glimpses the finish line, it knows exactly where it has to go and how to get there. Once this team got to the Stanley Cup Final, the players could see it. They were determined to win that series, and they wanted to win at home.

I felt really good about Game 6 after winning Game 5 in Tampa, though of course I never would have said that to anyone. You can never be overconfident. I was nervous until Patrick Kane scored with just over 5 minutes remaining in the game. When the puck found the back of the net after that great setup by Brandon Saad and pass from Brad Richards, I knew.

Celebrating out on the United Center ice, I thought of my dad, grandpa and uncle. I believe they were all looking down upon us and were really excited about winning the Stanley Cup in Chicago. We dreamed about it together for two decades, and I realize how fortunate we are as an organization to get to this level. Where we were no longer matters; what matters is how we got to where we are now and that we're never turning back.

We have worked relentlessly as a franchise to build the Blackhawks into a well-oiled machine. Some people talk about us being a dynasty, but dynasties usually involve the same group of players. Because of the NHL's salary cap, our past three Stanley Cup teams have all been different. Just like the group on the ice, we are always evolving off it. But the nucleus is constant; that core group has been here for it all.

So much of our success is due to this nucleus. What sets us apart is our experience and resolve. Losing the way we did to the Los Angeles Kings in the 2014 playoffs—in Game 7 on home ice—left a bad taste in our mouths. We came into this season knowing we had to work that much harder, and we rose to the occasion.

Vice President/General Manager Stan Bowman has always said that the first round of the playoffs is the most difficult. I agree with him, especially after what we went through in this year's opening round. The guys had to dig deep against Nashville, especially during those overtime games. The Game 1 comeback win in triple OT set the stage for the rest of our playoff run. That first victory was when I recognized that there was something special about this group, this season.

But it was early. We still had three rounds and three strong opponents to overcome.

The Nashville and Anaheim series were both very tough, physically and mentally. However, the core group had been in this position before. Being tested only motivated them further.

During the last minute of Game 6 against Tampa, my daughter Lizzy, who was sitting next to me, said, "You know, Dad, we're going to win this thing." I looked at the clock and there were exactly 17 seconds left.

After those fateful, triumphant 17 seconds in 2013 against Boston, I knew nothing was for certain until the final horn sounded.

And when it did, the crowd exploded.

The celebration that started that Monday night and continued throughout the summer was tremendous. I happened to be on the bus that was carrying the Cup during the parade, and the roar was deafening as it passed by the crowds along the route. We were riding through the open air of downtown Chicago, but the sound was like being inside the United Center when the Blackhawks score a goal.

The rally that the city put on for us at Soldier Field was remarkable. The noise, the crescendo, the sea of red—it was a spectacular sight. The most important part, though, was that we were able to truly share this championship with our fans. ▥

OPPOSITE: Rocky Wirtz and his grandson, Lachlan, enjoy some time together with the Stanley Cup.

A DREAM FULFILLED

by JOHN F. MCDONOUGH, PRESIDENT AND CEO

Of the three Stanley Cup championships the Blackhawks have brought to Chicago in the past six seasons, this one was the most impactful. It took the franchise 77 years to do it, but we finally accomplished something that few teams have.

We won at home.

The euphoria that engulfed the United Center that Monday night in June exceeded my wildest expectations. During the revelry, you're looking around at your family, friends, coworkers and the players embracing one another on the ice. You see the thousands of adoring fans, the building bursting at the seams. Some are crying; some are screaming. But they're all happy. All of them.

It almost seemed like a dream. It still does.

I've had moments over the last few months where I'll be at a restaurant or mall and someone will recognize me and say, "Congratulations!" I have to pause for a second and smile. Wow, have we really won three?

Like in 2010 and 2013, I took the Cup to where I was born and raised, Edison Park on Chicago's northwest side. I never imagined seeing thousands of people flood the middle of Northwest Highway. But I've also never seen anything as magnetic and charismatic as the Stanley Cup. It stops people in their tracks. They just want to get close to it, to touch it.

One thing I've learned over the years is that when you're lucky enough to have the Cup—or on the rare occasions when you wear your championship ring—you take it for someone else, you wear it for someone else, not for you.

Those experiences are overwhelming and humbling. But after all the hysteria and hoopla passes, we come right back to what we talk about here all the time: sustaining it. Sustaining this success. Making the playoffs and putting yourself in a position to compete for the Stanley Cup.

Making it gives you a chance. That's really all you need.

We've given ourselves a chance in seven straight seasons, with five Western Conference Final appearances along the way. That process has required patience and a lot of collaboration. Not too long ago, we were pushing ourselves just to get incrementally better every single day—then maybe after a couple years, we'd have a really solid organization. I certainly wasn't thinking about multiple Stanley Cup titles when Rocky Wirtz hired me after taking over as chairman in 2007; we just wanted to "get it right."

Now we have high expectations at 1901 West Madison Street, as we strive to improve and continue to move forward. Spending too much time reflecting on what we have achieved is counterproductive to our approach. We must always be prepared for the challenges and opportunities ahead.

That's why I've dispelled the notion of a dynasty from day one. There will never be a time when we take things for granted. Anaheim scored three goals in 37 seconds against us, so no lead is ever safe. Not until the final horn sounded in Game 6 against Tampa Bay did I let myself think it was over. That last minute felt like a week.

We're incredibly fortunate to have amazing players, a Hall of Fame coach in Joel Quenneville, a great owner in Rocky and a young, dynamic staff. Additionally, we're blessed with a fan base that has wildly embraced us. Every one of those millions of fans has had an influence on our winning three Stanley Cups.

It wasn't a dream. ☰

OPPOSITE: John McDonough and the Stanley Cup appear in Edison Park, where he was born and raised.

THE BLACKHAWKS WAY

CHAPTER ONE

THE BLACKHAWKS WAY

by BOB VERDI

Well before it was time for him to be introduced at another sold-out Blackhawks Convention this past July, Chairman Rocky Wirtz blushed as thousands of attendees packed into a giant ballroom at the Hilton Chicago began a familiar chant.

"ROC-KY! ROC-KY! ROC-KY!"

In virtually every precinct of the professional sports landscape, the phrase "beloved owner" is an oxymoron carved in stone. But with Rocky's Blackhawks, trendsetters par excellence, the mood is palpably different. Now with three Stanley Cups in six years, a franchise that was on life support not long ago is attached to some highfalutin language.

Golden Era. Dynasty. America's Team.

"It's almost embarrassing, but it is also gratifying," Wirtz said. "If you had told me when I took over that we would be where we are now, I'd have put the odds at a million to one.

"You know how it is when you get hooked on a soap opera? You can't wait for the next day's installment? That's what it's like with our amazing fans. They just can't get enough. Games, information, gear, Blackhawks TV. They just want more, year-round. Whether [or not] we're a dynasty, I know this: The New York Islanders and Edmonton Oilers won all those Cups in the '80s with basically the same team. We've had to make big changes, but because everybody is on board, we've kept on winning."

When National Hockey League Commissioner Gary Bettman, who oversaw the inception of an unforgiving salary cap designed to nourish parity, presented the 2015 Stanley Cup to the Blackhawks after they clinched with Corey Crawford's 2-0 whitewash of the Tampa Bay Lightning at the United Center on June 15, he uttered that word—"dynasty"—to a screaming-room-only crowd of 22,424. A few days later, the cover story of Sports Illustrated was about this "Modern Dynasty" in Chicago. Media outlets throughout the United States and Canada hailed the Blackhawks for their dominance through usually extenuating competitive circumstances.

Only President and CEO John McDonough, the conscience of a driven front office, waved a caution flag, albeit with a smile on his face.

"If people want to call us a dynasty, that's fine," McDonough said. "But you will never hear that from our staff or in our building. We are in the business of winning, and I don't want us to be measured over a relatively brief period of six years.

"I grew up with the Boston Celtics and UCLA basketball. The Detroit Red Wings have qualified for the playoffs in 24 consecutive seasons. No other team has a run like that going, in any league. That means they've had a chance to win the Stanley Cup in 24 straight seasons. This is what we want to do here with the Blackhawks. We want to give our fans a chance to have a Stanley Cup over decades and decades because that's what they deserve.

"That is our goal: continued excellence. That's why, although we celebrate today what our team has accomplished, we move on to do better the next day. We are humble but still hungry; proud but never satisfied. We are on a nice run, yes. It's a pretty good start."

The foundation for this "pretty good start" is an unyielding all-in-this-together mantra that results in what McDonough describes as almost a "collegial" atmosphere between the business side and hockey operations. Their responsibilities differ, but not their objectives, and it is apparent even from a distance.

"When I played here, the players were close," said Pat Stapleton, a star Blackhawks defenseman from 1965 to 1973. "But we were never close with management. There was a division between both sides. I sense that it's the complete opposite now."

Alas, there was no alternative when Wirtz assumed control of a moribund franchise in the fall of 2007, then decided he would not take no for an answer from McDonough, a decorated executive with the Cubs.

"I tip my hat to our players," said Executive Vice President Jay Blunk, who joined the Blackhawks a couple months later. "We were underdogs, and they embraced that mentality. We had to fight our way out of a deep, dark hole, and we didn't know whether we'd ever make it. When Duncan Keith and Brent Seabrook came here, the building was half empty. Then came Jonathan Toews and Patrick Kane. They too bought in. We had to be different—friendly, likable, accessible, out in the community.

"It was hard. We were off the radar. When Jonathan showed up, we had to correct some media. They pronounced his name 'Toes.' We had lost generations, but now, because of these guys, all those millennials love this team. Social media. Website. Our TV ratings are through the roof, and that doesn't count bars and restaurants where people gather to watch games like it's a civic event. We can't pay our players to come to the Convention

because it counts against the cap. But there's Toews and so many others because they feel an obligation. They feed off our fans at the United Center.

"Are we still underdogs after three Cups in six years? The culture has not changed. We had to get this organization out of the mud and onto the highway, and we have to make sure we never, ever slide back into the ditch. Our players are incredible not only on the ice, but off the ice. They connect with fans, and fans know it's genuine. From a standpoint of success and popularity, yes, there is a strong argument that this is the golden era for hockey in this city. But we still remember what it was like in that dark, deep hole."

Extraordinary players, extraordinary individuals have guided the Blackhawks to three Stanley Cups in six years, a golden era indeed for a franchise that won three Stanley Cups from 1926 to 2009.

ABOVE: A sea of fans rejoices as a parade bus carrying Blackhawks Chairman Rocky Wirtz, Brent Seabrook, Duncan Keith, Patrick Sharp and the Stanley Cup rolls by.
OPPOSITE: President and CEO John McDonough, Executive Vice President Jay Blunk and Wirtz celebrate in the locker room following Game 6 of the Stanley Cup Final.

"IF PEOPLE WANT TO CALL US A DYNASTY, THAT'S FINE,"
MCDONOUGH SAID. "BUT YOU WILL NEVER HEAR THAT
FROM OUR STAFF OR IN OUR BUILDING. WE'RE IN THE
BUSINESS OF WINNING, AND I DON'T WANT US TO BE
MEASURED OVER A BRIEF PERIOD OF SIX YEARS."

Keith, the longest-tenured Blackhawk, arrived in 2005. He recalls rows of unoccupied seats. Now the all-world defenseman has the 2015 Conn Smythe Trophy along with two Norris Trophies. Were he a mailman, he would be the one who would take a walk on his day off.

Seabrook, Keith's usual blue-line partner, is a rock, a leader now with a permanent letter on his sweater. He is the last guy out of the room for every period, a voice to be heard when he has something to say, a man with a penchant for scoring big goals at the biggest moments.

Toews, curator of an incredible shrinking bucket list, also owns two Olympic gold medals. As captain, he is among the greatest leaders in sports and arguably the most complete player in hockey. He could move his hardware into the garage, but then where does he put his car?

Kane, the magician, has hands of a surgeon. He makes the puck do what few others can. He was trending toward a Hart Trophy season until he was felled by a serious collarbone injury, but picked up where he left off in the playoffs with 23 points in 23 games. Is there a more electric performer in the NHL?

Marian Hossa, consummate professional, treats the puck as his pet. He protects it, cares for it, handles it passionately. In return, the loyal puck acts obediently. Should it stray, Hossa responds as though his pet has run away. A two-way maestro, Hossa will skate effortlessly into the Hall of Fame.

Niklas Hjalmarsson, the shutdown defenseman, is usually pitted against the best that adversaries have to offer. He would rather stick his face in front of a puck than a camera because he eschews calling attention to himself. "It's a Swedish thing," he says.

Crawford is the Rodney Dangerfield of goalies, except in his locker room, where teammates ooze respect. He did not play in 2010, but could have earned the 2013 Conn Smythe Trophy, as recipient Kane volunteered. Brilliant in the 2015 Final against Tampa Bay, the NHL's highest-scoring team, all Crawford does is win.

With this core, complemented by additions from the minors or other organizations, the Blackhawks have appeared in five conference championships and contested 117 playoff games since Joel Quenneville was appointed head coach early in the 2008-09 season. The product has been consistently appealing to the masses.

"They're the most popular team in the country," said Tony Esposito, the Blackhawks' Hall of Fame ambassador. "You would think it would level off at some point, but it only keeps growing. There's never been anything like it in this city."

Bobby Hull echoed Tony O's sentiment.

"I remember when we played and we were the toughest ticket in town," said "The Golden Jet," also a Hall of Fame ambassador. "But it wasn't like this. I always believed we were in the entertainment business, and so do these guys. It takes a lot to get me excited, but I get excited watching these Blackhawks. Not only Toews and Kane, but guys like Andrew Shaw. What is he, 165 pounds? Half of that is heart."

The Blackhawks have logged 329 consecutive sellouts at the United Center since the last vacant chair was seen there in the spring of 2008. Their wait list for tickets is 18,000 and counting. They attract more fans on the road than they used to at home, and that includes Canada, where hockey is gospel, where fans appreciate visiting teams that play with style, panache and élan.

But it is worth noting that even *before* the Stanley Cup conquest in 2010, the new brand was being established. Citing enlightened management, Forbes toasted the Blackhawks for effecting "The Greatest Sports-Business Turnaround Ever." That was in May 2009.

OPPOSITE AND ABOVE: That magic moment! Andrew Shaw, Corey Crawford, Jonathan Toews, Marian Hossa and the United Center crowd go crazy after the game clock hits zero.

"THE CULTURE HAS NOT CHANGED," BLUNK SAID. "WE HAD TO GET THIS ORGANIZATION OUT OF THE MUD AND ONTO THE HIGHWAY, AND WE HAVE TO MAKE SURE WE NEVER, EVER SLIDE BACK INTO THE DITCH."

"We had a flawed structure," Wirtz said. "Our payroll 10 years ago wasn't that low, but Chicago was the only place we were spending money. We didn't spend on scouting, development and coaching anywhere else. We have apartment buildings in our corporation that were built in the 1930s. But you can't just milk them. You have to upgrade, modernize, all the time. We weren't doing that with our hockey team.

"We had to overpay free agents to come here, and they were 35, past their primes. We lacked a plan and personnel. Now the NHL has a salary cap. It hurts to lose players, but it forces you to develop new ones, young players who keep you from becoming old and stale. Plus, there is no salary cap on hiring quality front office people to help get you where you want to go. Now we pay attention to what's happening with our farm club in Rockford, not just what's happening in Chicago. Fans didn't like us years ago. They liked hockey and the players, but management, not so much. I can't blame them."

The organization's commitment to winning was underscored in late February when Kane incurred a serious collarbone injury. Because of his projected long-term rehabilitation, the Blackhawks received salary cap relief. They could have sat tight and lowered any expectation of a Stanley Cup that year. Instead, Vice President/General Manager Stan Bowman aggressively pursued and traded for center Antoine Vermette from the Arizona Coyotes, defenseman Kimmo Timonen from the Philadelphia Flyers and winger Andrew Desjardins from the San Jose Sharks. These moves cost the Blackhawks players and draft choices, plus money. Kane still drew his salary, but the new players also had to be paid.

"That sent a huge message to our locker room," Toews recalled. "The front office was still behind us. They believed in us, even if Kaner was going to be out for a while. I couldn't believe we got Antoine Vermette. He was the premier free agent available at the deadline. And we got him."

Wirtz was not even consulted.

"No need," he said. "It meant maybe three more paychecks for Vermette. We don't put handcuffs on Stan."

Bowman presented his plan.

"He always has one," McDonough said. "We went over every aspect of Kane's injury, the timetable for his return and what we could do to reinforce what we had. Stan and his staff—Vice President of Hockey Operations Al MacIsaac, Assistant General Manager Norm Maciver— knew exactly what they wanted to do and why. Vermette was the guy, and they got him."

Vermette scored three game-winners in the playoffs, including two in the Final. He has returned to the Coyotes, but he has his name on the Cup.

"We paid the price to rent Vermette," Bowman said. "Rocky is the best."

Alas, the intransigent salary cap did not bend for the 2015 champions, as was the case in 2010 and 2013. Gone are Patrick Sharp, an alternate captain whose core contributions to three Cups are inestimable; Brandon Saad, a young and strong frontline forward; and Johnny Oduya, a top-four defenseman who swallowed heavy minutes during the marathon playoff run of 23 games, which included 11 overtime periods.

"It's a tough and unfortunate part of the industry," Bowman said. "Patrick came here in 2005 and was an

2014-2015 CHICAGO BLACKHAWKS

TOP ROW (left to right): Kevin LeClair, Andrew Desjardins, A.J. Dolan, Sara Bailey, Mike Dorsch, Andrew LeFevour, Matt Brooks, Niklas Hjalmarsson, Brian Higgins, Michael Terry, Brian Dahm, Anthony Stefani, Bryan Bickell, Brian Howe, Mike Gapski, Kevin Orris, Marian Hossa, Jim Gary, Nick Zombolas, John Wiedeman, Ryan Gallante, Jeff Thomas, Spencer Montgomery, Michal Rozsival, Sean Grady

FOURTH ROW (left to right): Jim Heintzelman, Troy Parchman, Eric Lear, Antoine Vermette, Kelly Keogh, Brian Szubryck, Steve DiLenardi, Allison Ferrara, Troy Murray, Brad Richards, Greg Zinsmeister, Sean Keefer, David Rundblad, Judd Sirott, John Sandberg, Joakim Nordstrom, Amber Hughes, Andrew Roan, T.R. Johnson, Daniel Cardillo, Neil Desmond, Joe Doyle, Brandon Saad, Paul Unruh, Kyle Davidson, Ian Gentile

THIRD ROW (left to right): Maggie Paoli, Amber Fry, Shannon Pyrz, Johnny Oduya, Julie Lowins, Lauren O'Brien, Marcus Kruger, Jake Tuton, Leah Hendrickson, Patricia Walsh, Andrew Shaw, Hudson Chodos, Kelly Smith, Shilpa Rupani, Kris Versteeg, Danny Wyse, Ashley Hinton, Molly Connelly, Kimmo Timonen, Kyleen Howe, Teuvo Teravainen, Austin Hunt, Andrew Contis, Pawel Prylinski, D.J. Kogut

SECOND ROW (left to right): James Bare, Pat Foley, Patrick Sharp, Rebecca Goldstein, Kayla Kindred, Bob Verdi, Brent Seabrook, Adam Rogowin, Laura Clawson, Meghan Bower, Elizabeth Queen, Annie Camins, Patrick Kane, Jillian Smith, Leanne Mayville, Lauren Peterson, Duncan Keith, Dan Rozenblat, Emerald Gao, Stephanie Dubin, Leah Pascarella, Marie Sutera, Paul Goodman, Jeff Uyeno

FRONT ROW (left to right): Scott Darling, Matt Meacham, Peter Hassen, Brandon Faber, Adam Kempenaar, Mike Kitchen, Norm MacIver, Scotty Bowman, Joel Quenneville, Stan Bowman, Rocky Wirtz, Jonathan Toews, John McDonough, Jay Blunk, Al Macisaac, Kevin Dineen, Chris Werner, Mark Bernard, Tony Ommen, T.J. Skattum, Steve Waight, Jimmy Waite, Corey Crawford

NOT PICTURED: Chase Agnello-Dean, Kevin Delaney, Lindsay Dresser, Eddie Olczyk, Antti Raanta, Kathie Raimondi, Trevor van Riemsdyk, Anna Warner

integral part of our success in every way. Brandon is a great player, and we hated to lose him. But he sought a long-term contract and, at the time, we were only able to propose a short-term contract. Johnny was also terrific and a veteran presence, but again, we just could not fit him under the cap.

"You have to be nimble in this business. When you make a deal and can't take on salary, you try for draft picks. Or you can flip those draft picks for players. Instead of another team tendering Saad an offer sheet that would have brought us draft picks, we got players—good players—from the Columbus Blue Jackets. Same with Patrick and the Dallas Stars. Johnny was unrestricted, and he signed there for something we weren't able to give, as much as we would have liked to.

"I know some fans are upset about the guys we couldn't keep, but our job is to manage our assets. You can't have a full team on the Blackhawks plus a full team of prospects that are all untouchable. You want your favorites to play here for 15 years, and some will. But you have to deal with reality, and one covenant we have is that we must prepare for our future. We still have great core players, and now, if you're a young guy trying to make our roster, you see what they've done. This is a place where you can win Stanley Cups."

The offseason machinations jolted the regulars, of course. But as Toews offered, "Whether it's this year or down the road, we have that culture and we have that identity, that belief in our room. There's no doubt, and we're not done yet."

En route to the 2015 Stanley Cup, the Blackhawks accumulated press clippings, but did not have the urge or time to digest them.

"Blackhawks Build a Juggernaut With Talent on Ice and in Front Office"—The New York Times.

"The Blackhawks are doing everything we could ask of them—as a business, as members of the community, but most of all as a hockey team, as a dynasty in full force. The bandwagon can't be called a bandwagon anymore. It's too big."—The Wall Street Journal.

During the Final, Hall of Fame writer Kevin Allen of USA Today authored a piece under a headline fans in Chicago thought they might never see: "Lightning covet Blackhawks' blueprint."

If you remember that dark, deep hole, rub your eyes and read that again. If you're new to the Blackhawks, enjoy and anticipate more of the same.

From no way to the Blackhawks Way.

From a Model T to The Model.

From dead ends to parade routes. ▮

OPPOSITE: Marian Hossa hoists the Stanley Cup before a packed Soldier Field crowd.

CHASING HISTORY

CHAPTER TWO

ICONIC NIGHTS AND MILESTONES

by LEAH PASCARELLA

Six months before embarking on their historic 2015 Stanley Cup championship run, the Blackhawks began the regular season knowing they had a formidable core, but realizing they would be facing 29 foes with the same hopes—and some with similar talent. It might have seemed like a lifetime ago, but the regular season had its share of iconic nights and milestone moments. From rookies to veterans, everyone played their parts, whether in front of a perpetually sold-out United Center crowd or braving the elements in a picturesque outdoor setting. Here's a look back at the winter of 2014-15—the preamble to the storm.

DREAM DEBUT

The Oct. 26 game against the Ottawa Senators was not an ordinary night for the Blackhawks. For starters, it was their annual Hockey Fights Cancer Night, when children who are battling cancer participate in a ceremonial puck drop. Additionally, Lemont, Ill., native Scott Darling made his NHL debut and became the first Blackhawks goaltender to win an inaugural appearance at the United Center after stopping 32 of 33 shots. Darling wasn't the only player to dazzle the crowd in the Blackhawks' 2-1 win over the Senators; early in the second period, Patrick Kane earned his 500th career point with an assist on a goal by Jonathan Toews, joining Denis Savard as the second Blackhawk to reach the 500-point mark in his first seven seasons.

STORYBOOK NIGHT

Marian Hossa was hoping that Oct. 30 would be a special occasion. He was sitting on 998 career points entering that night's game, which coincidentally was to be his 1,100th NHL contest, and he had a feeling it could happen in Ottawa, where he started his NHL career after being drafted in the first round by the Senators in 1997. Hossa started the night off with an assist on Toews' goal in the first period. Late in the third period, he received the puck below the goal line and wrapped it around the net and past the goaltender to reach the 1,000-point mark. The classy veteran became the 80th NHL player in history to reach this milestone, and he did it in storybook fashion.

CAPTAIN AND CROW

On Nov. 4, the Blackhawks made the trip to Bell Centre in Montreal to take on the Canadiens, and Toews made it an early celebration, opening the scoring with his 200th NHL goal; he later assisted on Kane's goal in the third period for his 450th career point. Additional goals from Marcus Kruger, Brad Richards and Kris Versteeg gave the Blackhawks a comfortable 5-0 win. The team had an especially happy goalie as Corey Crawford authored a 28-save shutout in his hometown.

HELPING HAND

He might have been a new arrival last season, but Richards began his career long before he landed in the Windy City. On Nov. 16, Richards stepped onto the ice at the United Center for his 1,000th NHL game, to be played against a former team in the Dallas Stars. The 34-year-old center was honored with a silver stick in a pregame ceremony with his family as he received a lively round of applause for his accomplishments. Richards didn't net a goal during the matchup, but he did tally two assists on goals by Kane and Versteeg. His helpers were the 598th and 599th of his career, and aided the team as they completed a 6-2 victory over the Stars.

FOLEY ENTERS HALL

It's hard to beat catching a game at the United Center, but fans watching at home would agree that cheering on the Blackhawks from their couches isn't so bad either, thanks to the Blackhawks' beloved TV play-by-play man, Pat Foley. Foley's passion for hockey and distinguished broadcasting career, including 32 years calling Blackhawks games, landed him a spot in the Hockey Hall

OPPOSITE: "...that our flag was still there!" Fans assist anthem singer Jim Cornelison at the 2014-15 home opener.

of Fame on Nov. 17. He spoke upon accepting the Foster Hewitt Memorial Award, but instead of congratulating himself, Foley thanked those who made his dream possible. He began his broadcasting career at just 26 years old and still considers himself "the luckiest guy in the world" to be able to call games for the best team in the league. "When I first started thinking of being a sports broadcaster as a very young man, I was hoping I would somehow wind up with a big-league team in a big-league town. So how did that work out?"

MILE-HIGH MILESTONE

Nearing the end of their annual "Circus Trip," the Blackhawks stopped at Pepsi Center to face the Colorado Avalanche on Nov. 26. Crawford started his 12th consecutive game, registering 29 saves in the Blackhawks' 3-2 win over the Avalanche. Kane may have been the star of the game, assisting on all three Blackhawks goals, but defenseman Brent Seabrook was the one who reached an important milestone, notching an assist on Toews' redirected goal for his 300th career point.

ALL IN

On Dec. 11, the Blackhawks won their season-best eighth straight, topping the Boston Bruins 3-2 at TD Garden. Darling made 32 saves in his third consecutive start, but with Toews exiting early after taking a dangerous hit, the Blackhawks' depth had to carry them through. Klas Dahlbeck, Ben Smith and Kane each produced a goal in the win, and Kruger came up with two assists.

SHARP ATTACK

The Blackhawks ended 2014 on a high note, and Patrick Sharp reached another career mark as Chicago hosted Central Division rival Nashville in a roller-coaster ride of a game on Dec. 29. Chicago ultimately prevailed 5-4 on a shootout goal by Toews. Trailing 3-0 in the second period, Richards, Andrew Shaw and Hossa sparked the Blackhawks offense to tie it up. Halfway through the second, Sharp got the puck to the net, and the always scrappy Shaw was there to finish off the play, giving Sharp his 500th NHL point. Bryan Bickell came up with a big tying goal with 1:13 left in regulation before Toews sealed the win.

PATRICK CONNECTION

Head Coach Joel Quenneville and Kane each had a special moment on Jan. 20, when the Blackhawks hosted the Arizona Coyotes. Q helmed his 500th game as Chicago's bench boss, a 6-2 win in which the Blackhawks shot out of the gate and never looked back. Toews opened the scoring, followed by Shaw and Kane, who capitalized on a rebound for his 200th NHL goal. Sharp picked up a helper on the play—nothing new for the veteran, who also assisted on Kane's first and 100th career tallies.

DUCK HUNT

On Jan. 30, the Blackhawks made their second trip to Honda Center to take on the conference-leading Anaheim Ducks. The Blackhawks were victorious when the two teams clashed in November, and Chicago was able to repeat the victory, smothering the Ducks in a 4-1 win. Kane posted two goals and an assist, and Sharp tied a career high with four assists. Additionally, Keith netted the game-winner with a close-range slap shot in the second, reaching the 400-point plateau in his career.

ELITE COMPANY

The Blackhawks know all too well that it can take 60 (or more) minutes to defeat the Winnipeg Jets, and that certainly was the case on Feb. 6. Winnipeg went up 1-0 early, but an explosive goal from Kane tied the game in the second period to give Quenneville hope for reaching the 300-win mark that night. Kane then found Brandon Saad late in overtime for the winner, making that hope a reality. Coach Q became just the second coach after Scotty Bowman, the Blackhawks' senior advisor to hockey operations, to win 300 games with two different teams.

DEBUTANTE BALL

The Blackhawks welcomed two new faces in their tilt against the Carolina Hurricanes on March 2. Trade-deadline acquisitions Kimmo Timonen and Antoine Vermette donned Blackhawks sweaters for the first time, receiving a warm Chicago welcome in a 5-2 win at the United Center. Toews led the team with two goals and an assist, and the new Blackhawks each logged a considerable amount of time: Timonen clocked in at 17:29, and Vermette skated 12:55.

OPPOSITE TOP: Marian Hossa is all smiles after registering his 1,000th point in Ottawa, where his illustrious career began.
OPPOSITE BOTTOM: Pat Foley accepts the Foster Hewitt Memorial Award for "outstanding contributions as a hockey broadcaster" during a ceremony in Toronto in November.

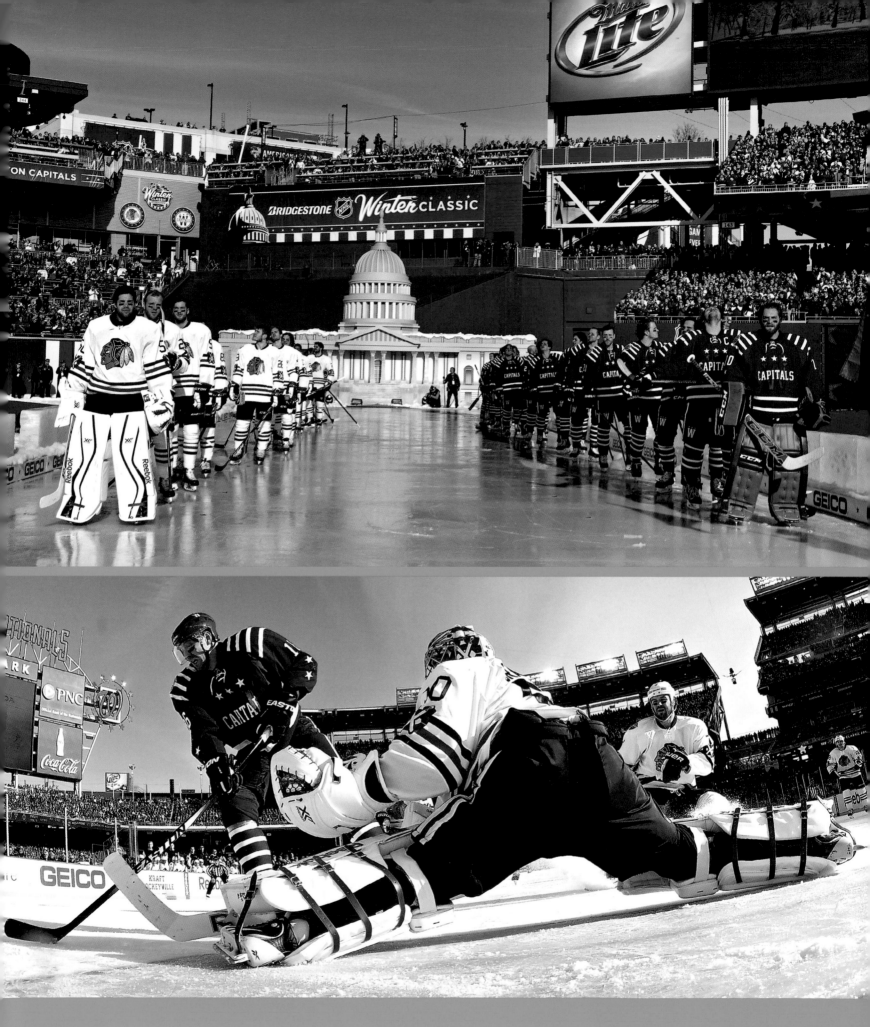

OPPOSITE TOP: Andrew Shaw poses for a picture after practicing with the USA Warriors hockey team on the eve of the 2015 Winter Classic in Washington, D.C.
OPPOSITE BOTTOM: Jonathan Toews and Marian Hossa share a lighthearted moment in the locker room before the Winter Classic.
ABOVE TOP: The players stand for the national anthem on a replica of the Potomac River at Nationals Park.
ABOVE BOTTOM: Corey Crawford stretches but can't quite make the save against Eric Fehr, who scored unassisted in the first.

ABOVE TOP: Scott Darling records one of his 25 saves in a dominant Madison Square Garden debut.
ABOVE BOTTOM: Brad Richards salutes the crowd after being honored prior to his 1,000th career NHL game.
OPPOSITE TOP: Fans voted in a league-leading five Blackhawks for the 2015 NHL All-Star Game in Columbus.
OPPOSITE BOTTOM: Bryan Bickell roars after scoring the game-tying goal against Nashville on Dec. 29.

STEALING THE SHOW

March 6 wasn't just any other Friday night, as the Blackhawks hosted the Edmonton Oilers in a nail-biter. The visitors struck first, but Seabrook tied the game at 1-1 with his eighth goal of the season. The score would stay there through 60 minutes and overtime, as Crawford made some key saves to get the Blackhawks to a shootout. Vermette put away the game-deciding goal in his second tilt with the Blackhawks, but it was Crawford's effort that fans went home talking about. The goaltender stopped a regular-season career-high 46 shots and denied all three Edmonton shooters in the tiebreaker.

SHUTOUT AT MSG

The Blackhawks traveled to Madison Square Garden on March 18 to take on the East-leading New York Rangers. The eventual 1-0 victory was extra special for Richards, who scored the game-winner against his previous team late in the game. Darling returned to the net for the first time in seven games and recorded his first NHL shutout with 25 saves, including 10 in the final 20 minutes as the Rangers fought to even the score. "You can't ask for much more," Darling said after completing a personal milestone in an iconic building against an Original Six foe.

TWO IS BETTER THAN ONE

Chicago's 3-1 win over the Hurricanes on March 23 was a big night for the coach and his captain. Goals in the first period from Shaw and Sharp gave the Blackhawks control of the game early, and Crawford was in top form, making 43 saves in the win. With under a minute left in the third period, Carolina pulled its goalie, and Shaw netted his second of the night with an assist from Toews, marking the captain's 500th NHL point. It may not have been the prettiest game, requiring 25 blocked shots, but the staunch defensive effort was enough to give Quenneville his 750th career victory.

DOWN TO THE WIRE

The Blackhawks needed a second gear to grind out a victory against the Jets on March 29. The back-and-forth game was tied 3-3 in the third period, thanks to goals from Shaw, Richards and Sharp. Late in the contest the Blackhawks found a way through. With 30 seconds left

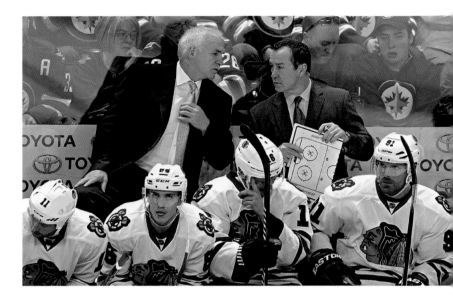

in regulation, Niklas Hjalmarsson fired a shot on goal, and Toews was able to tip it in to give the Blackhawks a 4-3 victory. Quenneville later called the win "our most important victory of the season," especially with crucial playoff positioning at stake.

D ON O

The Blackhawks hosted the defending Stanley Cup champion Los Angeles Kings on March 30, and the 4-1 victory was heavily influenced by the team's defensive corps. Keith's power-play tally early in the second period broke a 1-1 tie, and Hjalmarsson posted his 100th career point with his third goal of the season just 64 seconds later, giving the Blackhawks a commanding 3-1 lead. Despite not making the scoresheet, Johnny Oduya ended the game with two shots on goal and three hits, including a particularly heavy blow to Kings blueliner Jake Muzzin.

POSTSEASON-BOUND

With six games remaining in the regular season, the Blackhawks knew they needed to come out strong in their April 2 matchup against the Vancouver Canucks. Rookie Teuvo Teravainen opened the scoring for Chicago, and Toews and Kruger followed with a goal each in the third period. Crawford did his part as well, acrobatically denying the Canucks several times while making 35 saves on the night. The Blackhawks clinched a playoff berth for the seventh straight season with the 3-1 victory, establishing their first such postseason stretch since 1997. ▥

OPPOSITE TOP: Kimmo Timonen and Antoine Vermette played their first games as Blackhawks against the Hurricanes on March 2.
OPPOSITE BOTTOM: Niklas Hjalmarsson stick-pumps after posting his 100th career point against the Kings on March 30.
ABOVE: Head Coach Joel Quenneville called the March 29 win against the Jets "our most important victory of the season."

ABOVE TOP: A wish come true—Jordan King of Belvidere, Ill., gets advice from his favorite player, Jonathan Toews, at a practice.
ABOVE BOTTOM: Gabriel Colon from Algonquin, Ill., prepares to take the ice at practice thanks to the Make-a-Wish Foundation.
OPPOSITE TOP: The Blackhawks wore purple warmup jerseys in honor of Hockey Fights Cancer Night on Oct. 26.
OPPOSITE BOTTOM: The Blackhawks partnered with the Make-a-Wish and Bear Necessities Pediatric Cancer foundations for a special pregame on-ice ceremony recognizing five local children.

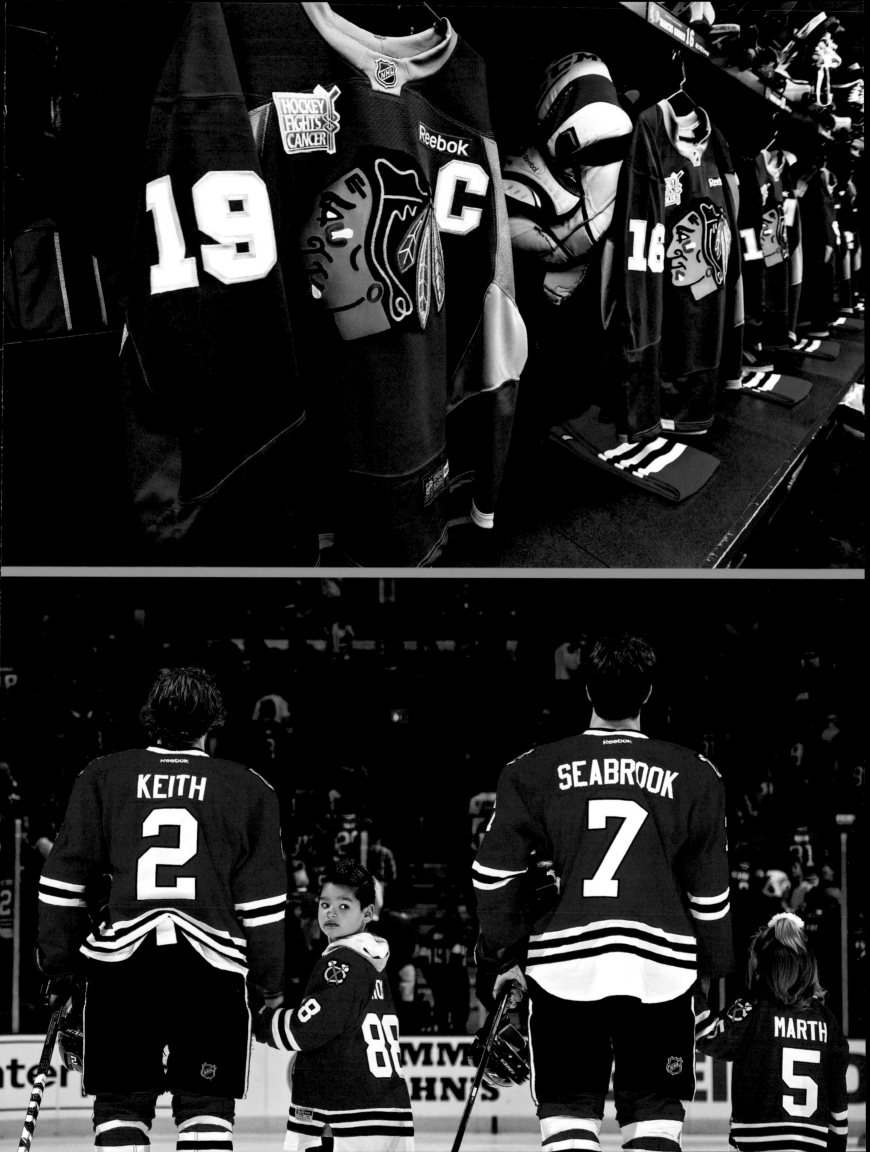

OPPOSITE TOP: Kimmo Timonen and Andrew Desjardins congratulate Teuvo Teravainen after his goal on April 2.
OPPOSITE BOTTOM: Corey Crawford stopped all three Edmonton attempts in the shootout in a 2-1 win on March 6.
ABOVE TOP: I'm on a boat! Bryan Bickell, Andrew Shaw, Jonathan Toews and Scott Darling goof around on the ferry to Alcatraz Island during the Father-Son Road Trip.
ABOVE BOTTOM: Shaw mocks his dad, Doug, and Bryan Bickell's dad, Bill, as they catch some z's on the flight to Arizona.

WHAT'S YOUR GOAL?

by **ADAM KEMPENAAR**

Like most successful endeavors, it began simply enough.

When Chairman Rocky Wirtz hired John McDonough as president of the Blackhawks in late 2007, McDonough had a singular focus. "He said, 'This team has one goal—to be the best, to be a Stanley Cup contender every year,'" explained Pete Hassen, Blackhawks senior executive director of marketing. "We took that objective to our agency, Ogilvy & Mather, and they ran with it."

Or, more appropriately, *skated* with it. Fans may remember the very first "One Goal" television spots featuring various Blackhawks players skating up to a microphone. "My goal…is to top that one," said a then-precocious young captain Jonathan Toews as a highlight-reel goal from his rookie season looped on a nearby TV.

"In evolving the campaign, we realized there were only so many ways guys can say they want to win," Ogilvy Group Creative Director Dave Metcalf recalled. "We thought, what if we just add a simple question to the end?"

What's your goal?

"We didn't know what was going to happen, or if we were going to get any responses at all," Metcalf said.

But Ogilvy and the Blackhawks did get responses. Several thousand of them, in fact, poured in over social media in the form of Facebook posts, tweets and videos. It quickly became clear that the next logical step was to try to fulfill some of the goals—and do it in surprising ways.

Christina DeVries, 16, who is blind and hindered by several health issues, wanted to experience the atmosphere of a Blackhawks game live at the United Center. So during a game in December, there was Christina, being ushered in through the players' entrance, then greeted by Patrick Sharp, who took her out onto the ice for a quiet moment before the arena swelled with the crashes, clangs and cheers of the game. Later, Christina joined the chorus of fans singing along to the anthem and visited John Wiedeman and Troy Murray in the WGN Radio booth.

Smiles, hugs and tears abounded for everyone involved, and for viewers, too.

"Our goal wasn't to make people cry," Metcalf said. "It was to make them feel uplifted after watching it."

Judging by the overwhelming reaction, including national TV time on ESPN's "SportsCenter" and coverage on a multitude of networks, websites, blogs and social platforms—mission accomplished.

Challenged by a rare neurological disorder that affects her speech and movement, Cammy Babiarz, 5, doesn't let Rett syndrome deter her from rooting for the Blackhawks. Her goal was to learn to skate and to score a goal with her favorite player, Duncan Keith.

"By that time, Duncan had seen the first couple of videos that we did, so he knew how it was going to play out," Metcalf said. "He's pretty competitive. He joked, 'I'm a much better actor than Sharpy, so it's no problem.'"

"Duncan being a dad and his son, Colton, being so important to him—those fatherly instincts came out right away," Hassen added.

But not all of the new spots—there were a total of seven last season—tried to pack such an emotional punch.

Alexis Waszczyk, 5, wanted her hockey hero, Toews, to buy some Girl Scout cookies. With an assist from Andrew Shaw, Alexis and her parents visited Toews at home, where the notoriously healthy eater couldn't resist such a sweet sales pitch. The video, a Blackhawks TV and Banner Collective production, concluded with Toews ironing a new patch on Alexis' vest. Well, *trying* to iron a new patch. The Blackhawks equipment managers may not be asking for Toews' assistance anytime soon, but Alexis was more than happy to trade a crooked patch for a once-in-a-lifetime experience.

"We say it all the time: We are lucky we work in hockey," Hassen said. "We have the best players in sports, no doubt about it. What you see in these ads, it's not scripted. We don't have to coach these guys. This is who they are, and it's why we appreciate everything that they do." ■

2014-2015 REGULAR SEASON

FINAL STATISTICS

PLAYER	POS	GP	G	A	PTS	+/-	PIM	PP	SH	GW	S	TOI
JONATHAN TOEWS	C	81	28	38	66	30	36	6	2	7	192	19:33
PATRICK KANE	RW	61	27	37	64	10	10	6	0	5	186	19:51
MARIAN HOSSA	RW	82	22	39	61	17	32	6	1	2	247	18:33
BRANDON SAAD	LW	82	23	29	52	7	12	2	0	6	203	17:15
DUNCAN KEITH	D	80	10	35	45	12	20	3	0	2	171	25:33
PATRICK SHARP	LW	68	16	27	43	-8	33	8	0	2	230	16:48
BRAD RICHARDS	C	76	12	25	37	3	12	2	0	3	199	14:53
KRIS VERSTEEG	LW	61	14	20	34	11	35	2	0	1	134	15:50
BRENT SEABROOK	D	82	8	23	31	-3	27	4	0	2	181	22:10
BRYAN BICKELL	LW	80	14	14	28	5	38	1	0	3	113	12:04
ANDREW SHAW	RW	79	15	11	26	-8	67	5	0	2	146	14:56
NIKLAS HJALMARSSON	D	82	3	16	19	25	44	0	0	1	97	21:53
MARCUS KRUGER	C	81	7	10	17	-5	32	0	0	1	126	13:05
DAVID RUNDBLAD	D	49	3	11	14	17	12	0	0	1	58	12:47
MICHAL ROZSIVAL	D	65	1	12	13	0	22	0	0	0	56	17:00
JOHNNY ODUYA	D	76	2	8	10	5	26	0	0	0	76	20:17
BEN SMITH	RW	61	5	4	9	-1	2	0	0	0	77	13:35
TEUVO TERAVAINEN	C	34	4	5	9	4	2	0	0	1	66	12:47
DANIEL CARCILLO	LW	39	4	4	8	3	54	0	0	0	42	8:11
ANTOINE VERMETTE	C	19	0	3	3	-2	6	0	0	0	24	14:03
JOAKIM NORDSTROM	LW	38	0	3	3	-5	4	0	0	0	42	10:58
ANDREW DESJARDINS	LW	13	0	2	2	1	7	0	0	0	16	11:59
ADAM CLENDENING	D	4	1	1	2	1	2	1	0	0	2	13:10
PETER REGIN	C	4	0	1	1	1	0	0	0	0	3	8:20
MICHAEL PALIOTTA	D	1	0	1	1	0	0	0	0	0	2	12:45
KLAS DAHLBECK	D	4	1	0	1	-1	2	0	0	0	4	10:23
TREVOR VAN RIEMSDYK	D	18	0	1	1	0	2	0	0	0	21	13:32
KIMMO TIMONEN	D	16	0	0	0	-3	2	0	0	0	10	11:58
KYLE CUMISKEY	D	7	0	0	0	-1	0	0	0	0	5	13:17
TIM ERIXON	D	8	0	0	0	1	4	0	0	0	6	9:59
JEREMY MORIN	RW	15	0	0	0	0	15	0	0	0	28	7:44
PHILLIP DANAULT	C	2	0	0	0	0	0	0	0	0	2	9:30
RYAN HARTMAN	RW	5	0	0	0	-1	2	0	0	0	8	8:17
KYLE BAUN	RW	3	0	0	0	-1	0	0	0	0	4	12:32

GOALTENDER	GP	MIN	GAA	W-L	OT	SO	SA	GA	SV%	G	A	PIM
COREY CRAWFORD	57	3,333	2.27	32-20	5	2	1,661	126	.924	0	1	0
SCOTT DARLING	14	833	1.94	9-4	0	1	419	27	.936	0	0	0
ANTTI RAANTA	14	792	1.89	7-4	1	2	389	25	.936	0	0	0

"THERE ARE SO MANY BATTLES GOING ON....YOU GET TO ENJOY IT SOME NIGHTS. WE SHOULD BE HAPPY RIGHT NOW, CLINCHING THE PLAYOFF SPOT, BUT WE STILL HAVE SOME WORK TO DO."

— JOEL QUENNEVILLE

DREAMING IN COLOR

CHAPTER THREE

FIRST ROUND

by EMERALD GAO

April is the cruelest month, and the Nashville Predators can attest to that, after coasting through the first half of the season as the best team in the National Hockey League, only to be overtaken by St. Louis in the final weeks of the campaign, necessitating a first-round matchup with the Blackhawks. Nashville boss Peter Laviolette had an eager, skilled squad, headlined by rookie phenom Filip Forsberg, netminder Pekka Rinne and a boon of puck-moving talent on the blue line. A matchup against Joel Quenneville's experienced playoff juggernaut was almost guaranteed to produce a frenzied, vigorous series.

As in 2010, there was no easing into the postseason for Chicago against the Preds, who were young and fast and ferocious. Game 1 in Nashville began with a three-alarm fire, as the Predators fashioned three goals in the first period off a strong forecheck. After Scott Darling replaced Corey Crawford in net, the Blackhawks stirred to life, knotting the score before the end of the second.

With no time to let the nerves settle, Darling stood firm in his first career Stanley Cup Playoffs appearance—a record-setting outing that lasted 67:44, including a heart-stopping pad save on Ryan Ellis midway through the third period that drew a roar of wonder and dismay from the golden sea of Nashville faithful. Duncan Keith's game-winner in double overtime made Darling's 42 saves count, capping off "one of the greatest relief performances you're going to see," according to Quenneville.

Nashville tied the series with a 6-2 win in Game 2, netting three insurance goals in 139 seconds during the final period. But the victory came at a big cost, as captain Shea Weber left the game with a lower-body injury, adding to the loss of veteran center Mike Fisher in Game 1.

In an effort to quell Nashville's speedy transition game, Quenneville made a couple of depth changes ahead of Game 3 in Chicago. Antoine Vermette and Andrew Desjardins slid back into the lineup, and the latter made an immediate impact, opening the scoring for the Blackhawks in a 4-2 win. Darling, getting the nod in net, made 35 saves in what he later described as "the loudest stadium I've ever been a part of in my life," comprising over 22,000 local well-wishers.

In a series that couldn't have been devised by a hundred scriptwriters, Game 4 was the most dramatic chapter yet. By the end, the two teams combined for 100 shots on goal and 183 shot attempts as the clock ticked over from Tuesday to Wednesday—a marathon that was only briefly paused when the puck got lost in Rinne's gear during the second overtime. Shortly after midnight and a fifth intermission, Brent Seabrook's slapshot from the high slot found its way past a screened Rinne, inspiring Patrick Kane to try to lift him up, momentarily forgetting a physical difference of 4 inches and over 40 pounds.

Nashville would not go quietly into the offseason, however, and a Forsberg hat trick propelled the Preds to a 5-2 win in Game 5. That gave Chicago a chance to close out the series at the United Center, which they did, but not before one final plot twist.

Nashville dominated early and created leads of 2-0 and 3-1, leading to another goalie change—this time, Crawford exchanging positions with Darling. The Blackhawks fought back once again, getting the game-tying goal from Kane with just 6 seconds left in the first period. Then Keith, in an echo of his Game 1 winner, slapped the puck past Rinne from the left point late in regulation to close the book on Nashville.

It might not have been the tidiest effort, with Chicago struggling on the penalty kill and displaying an out-of-character propensity for giving up goals in bunches. Even as Quenneville praised his stars for rising to the occasion in a tightly contested series, he also recognized the need to improve: "We need to be better in all aspects of our game. We had a couple of bad starts—can't always give up 3-1, 3-0 leads and come back and win two games in the series. Hopefully that's a lesson." ◫

OPPOSITE: Jonathan Toews celebrates after scoring a first-period power-play goal in Game 6 of the First Round against Nashville.

GAME ONE
APRIL 15, 2015
W 4-3 (2OT)

In their very first contest of the 2015 Stanley Cup Playoffs, the Blackhawks proved the old adage: It's not how you start, but how you finish that matters. After falling in a 3-0 hole against the Predators, Head Coach Joel Quenneville didn't hesitate to make a bold change, swapping out Corey Crawford for Scott Darling to start the second period. The message got through, and Chicago evened the score with goals from Niklas Hjalmarsson, Patrick Sharp and Jonathan Toews before contesting a scoreless third and overtime that left fans of both teams breathless. In the second sudden death period, Duncan Keith took a slap shot that sailed through traffic and past Nashville goaltender Pekka Rinne, putting the final flourish on Darling's 42-save relief outing.

ABOVE TOP: Jonathan Toews celebrates Duncan Keith's winner against Nashville.
ABOVE BOTTOM: Scott Darling makes a stop on Roman Josi, one of 42 saves after relieving Corey Crawford.

GAME TWO
APRIL 17, 2015

L 6-2

The Predators had something to prove after losing a heartbreaker in Game 1 at Bridgestone Arena, and they did so with a big 6-2 win to even the series. Nashville and Chicago traded goals throughout the first half of the contest, but the Predators started the third period with a 3-2 lead and proceeded to go on a scoring spree. Filip Forsberg got the puck past Corey Crawford to ignite the charge; two more goals in the span of 139 seconds allowed Nashville to pull away with the victory. Despite a powerful showing from their opponents, the Blackhawks could take solace in the fact that they would return to Chicago with home-ice advantage in their pocket.

OPPOSITE TOP: Blackhawks fans show off their allegiance in the streets of Nashville during the First Round series.
OPPOSITE BOTTOM: Assistant Coach Mike Kitchen reviews game footage with Johnny Oduya before Game 2.
ABOVE TOP: Bryan Bickell and Mattias Ekholm clash on the ice at Bridgestone Arena.
ABOVE BOTTOM: Andrew Shaw battles for position in front of the Nashville net.

GAME THREE
APRIL 19, 2015
W 4-2

With the series tied at one game apiece, the Blackhawks looked to gain an edge in their first home game of the 2015 postseason. After sitting out Game 2, Scott Darling got his first career playoff start in the building he used to frequent as a fan and made the most of it to help Chicago nail down a 4-2 win. Newcomer Andrew Desjardins got the Blackhawks off to a promising start, scoring off an assist from Marian Hossa, but similar to Game 2, the momentum shifted back and forth between the two sides. In the end, goals from Brandon Saad and Brent Seabrook late in the second period, plus a 35-save performance from Darling, propelled the hometown team to victory.

OPPOSITE: Marian Hossa checks Victor Bartley into the glass.
ABOVE TOP: Scott Darling makes one of his 35 saves in his first career playoff start.
ABOVE BOTTOM LEFT: Andrew Desjardins celebrates his goal, which opened the scoring for Chicago.
ABOVE BOTTOM RIGHT: Corey Crawford congratulates Darling on his performance.

GAME FOUR
APRIL 21, 2015
W 3-2 (3OT)

Neither the Blackhawks nor their fans had any idea what they were in for when they arrived at the United Center on April 21. In a game that spanned 4 hours and 31 minutes, 101:00 of playing time and two calendar days, the Blackhawks outlasted the Predators 3-2 in front of a weary but spirited crowd. Brandon Saad evened the game at 2-2 in the third with his second goal in as many games, and Scott Darling's acrobatics kept the Blackhawks' hopes alive through two tense sudden-death periods. Shortly after midnight, Brent Seabrook scored the game-winner just one minute into in the third tiebreaker, then was buried under a pile of exhausted and grateful teammates. "I don't know if guys were excited I scored or excited the game was over," he said.

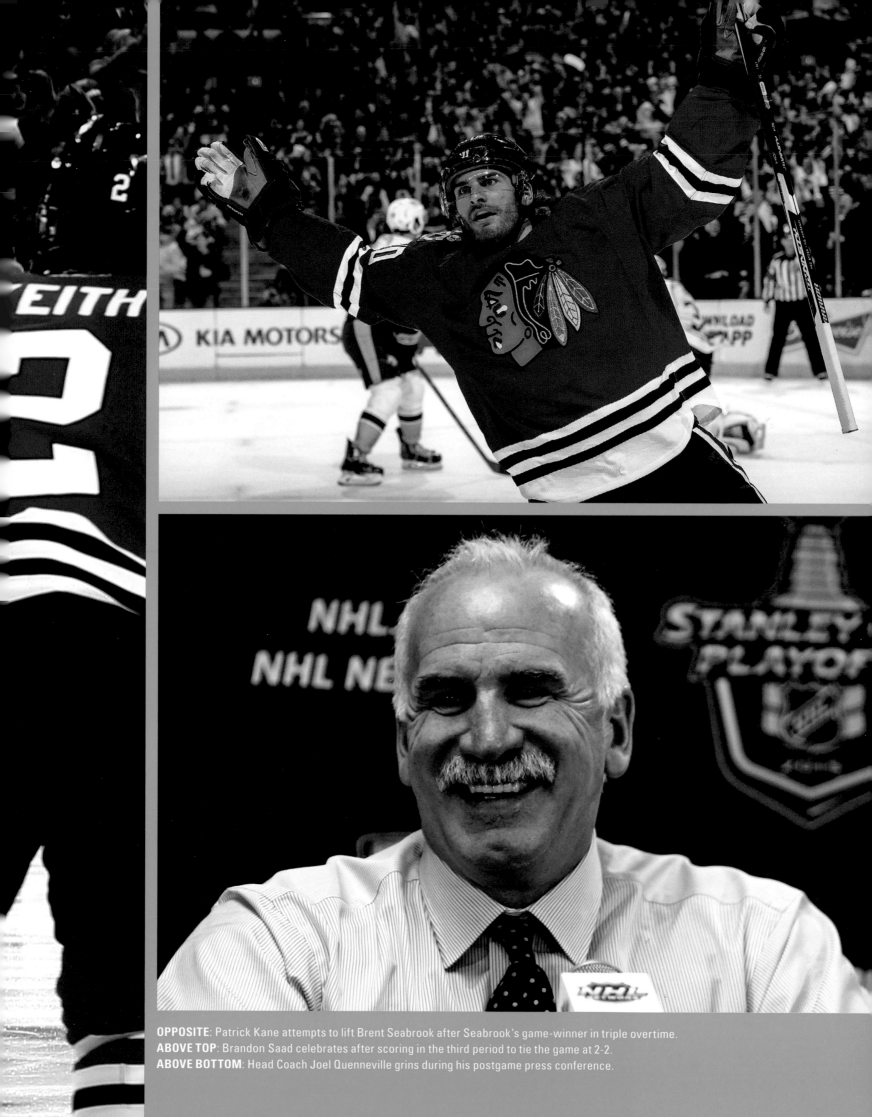

OPPOSITE: Patrick Kane attempts to lift Brent Seabrook after Seabrook's game-winner in triple overtime.
ABOVE TOP: Brandon Saad celebrates after scoring in the third period to tie the game at 2-2.
ABOVE BOTTOM: Head Coach Joel Quenneville grins during his postgame press conference.

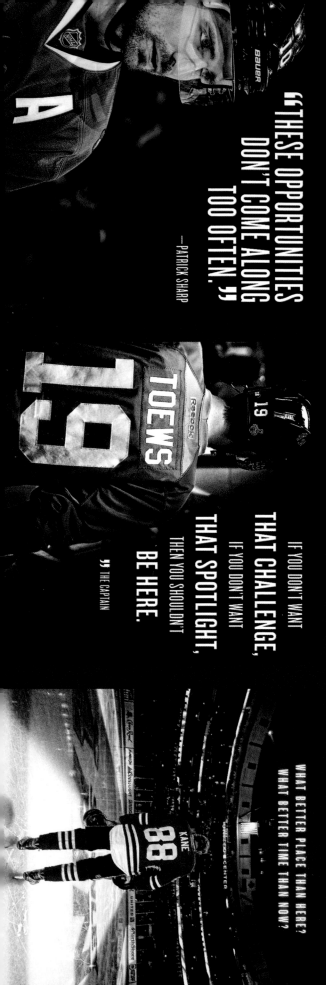

"
THERE'S NOTHING LIKE
COMING BACK HOME
AND PLAYING IN FRONT
OF YOUR FANS.

— PATRICK KANE

"THESE OPPORTUNITIES
DON'T COME ALONG
TOO OFTEN. "

— PATRICK SHARP

BECAUSE
IT'S
THE
CUP

IF YOU DON'T WANT
THAT CHALLENGE,
IF YOU DON'T WANT
THAT SPOTLIGHT,
THEN YOU SHOULDN'T
BE HERE.

" THE CAPTAIN

WHAT BETTER PLACE THAN HERE?
WHAT BETTER TIME THAN NOW?

WE HAVE A
GREAT OPPORTUNITY
HERE ON
HOME ICE.

— NIKLAS HJALMARSSON

" HE'S FAST
HE'S BIG
HE'S STRONG
HE'S DANGEROUS

—COACH Q

" NOBODY'S SATISFIED WITH JUST GETTING TO THE WESTERN CONFERENCE FINAL.

—DUNCAN KEITH **"**

WE'LL DO
WHATEVER
WE CAN TO
WIN IT.

- PATRICK SHARP

" WE WANT TO PLAY EVERY GAME LIKE IT'S A MUST-WIN. "

—JONATHAN TOEWS

" OUR FATE IS IN
OUR CONTROL. "

—JONATHAN TOEWS

IT'S GOING TO BE A
GREAT FEELING
STEPPING OUT THERE ON THE
UNITED CENTER ICE.

—MARCUS KRUGER

MR. CLUTCH

by **STEVE KONROYD, BLACKHAWKS TV STUDIO ANALYST**

as told to Eric Lear

At the biggest moments late in games, Brent Seabrook always seems to be the guy who steps up and delivers.

For me, it all started in October 2009, when the Blackhawks staged the most historic comeback in franchise history. They gave up five first-period goals to the Calgary Flames at the United Center before scoring five straight of their own. Then 26 seconds into overtime, Seabrook netted the game-winner.

Seabrook's overtime heroics were on display yet again in Game 4 of the 2015 opening round against Nashville. He beat Pekka Rinne with a blast from the high slot a minute into triple overtime, sending the Blackhawks faithful home happy and giving the team a commanding 3-1 series lead. That was the bruising defenseman's ninth career overtime game-winner, three of which have come in the postseason. I think that when you've done something once, it gives you the confidence and the belief that you can do it again. Seabrook has certainly shown time and time again that he can be counted on in key situations.

Even though goal-scoring isn't his forte, Seabrook's offense was on display throughout the 2015 championship run. He tallied seven postseason goals, a franchise record for defensemen in a playoff year. In my opinion, Seabrook has two great offensive weapons: He's got the heaviest shot on the team—Corey Crawford and Scott Darling both agree—and he recognizes, maybe more than anyone in the league, that any shot is a good shot.

In today's NHL, very rarely are you going to score with a clean shot from the point if the goalie sees it. Take a look at all of Seabrook's clutch game-winning goals. They come with bodies in front of the net—again, see that Game 4 winner against Nashville—or they're redirected, like his most famous overtime winner in Game 7 against the Detroit Red Wings to advance to the 2013 Western Conference Final.

Seabrook's offensive output and huge goals are great and will be remembered for years to come, but there's much more to his game. The Blackhawks have a number of players who are respected because of their speed and skill; Seabrook is a player who opponents respect for different reasons. At 6 feet, 3 inches and 220 pounds, he can play a punishing physical game. I think opposing forwards are acutely aware whenever he's on the ice.

We talk a lot about offensive defensemen—Ottawa's Erik Karlsson, for example—and defensive defensemen such as Niklas Hjalmarsson. Seabrook, along with his longtime partner Duncan Keith, fits into the category of two-way defensemen. When he has the puck, No. 7 can make a 150-foot pass and spring guys on breakaways. He can skate it out of his own end. He can make pretty plays and isn't lost when he doesn't have the puck. His on-ice awareness is second to none. He takes away ice in his own zone and very rarely gets beat in a one-on-one situation.

His heavy shot, physical play and two-way skills all make Seabrook a Blackhawk to be feared, yet that may not be his biggest contribution to this perennial championship club. Brent is one of the best leaders on the team, too. Again I think back to 2013 against Detroit, when Jonathan Toews got agitated and took three straight penalties in Game 4. Seabrook just skated over to the penalty box and coolly calmed down his visibly frustrated captain. We didn't get to hear what he said to Toews, but the gesture spoke volumes.

After 10 years in Chicago, the Blackhawks have bestowed Brent with the title of alternate captain. Whether he's wearing the "A" or not, though, he's always the same great leader. It's not about the name on the back or the letter on the front for Seabrook; it's all about the *logo* on the front. ▥

OPPOSITE: Following fist-bumps and motivational messages, Brent Seabrook is always the last player out of the dressing room.

GAME FIVE
APRIL 23, 2015
L 5-2

Arriving in Nashville for Game 5, the Blackhawks hoped to eliminate the Predators and move on to the next round of the playoffs, but the home team would not go down without a fight, taking a 5-2 victory and handing Scott Darling his first career postseason loss. Brad Richards opened the scoring at 13:27 of the first period, but Nashville quickly responded through Filip Forsberg. Three goals in the first 3:14 of the third period padded their lead, including another by Forsberg, and despite Kris Versteeg finding the back of the net late in the third, the Blackhawks weren't able to bounce back. Forsberg completed his first career NHL hat trick with an empty-netter to seal the win and give the Preds a glimmer of hope.

OPPOSITE TOP: Niklas Hjalmarsson, Scott Darling and Brandon Saad defend the net.
OPPOSITE BOTTOM: Antoine Vermette leaps into the air to clear a path for a shot.
ABOVE: Andrew Shaw stops by the bench during pregame warmups for his customary water spray.

GAME SIX
APRIL 25, 2015
W 4-3

The Blackhawks returned to Chicago for Game 6 still leading the series 3-2 and knowing they needed to take care of business at home. Scott Darling got his fourth consecutive start in net, but the Predators came out strong, getting two goals early and prompting Joel Quenneville to once again send a message to the bench—this time replacing Darling with Corey Crawford. The game picked up pace after that, and a total of six goals were scored in the first period, including a game-tying tally by Patrick Kane with just 6 seconds left in the frame. As he did in Game 1, defenseman Duncan Keith came up with the game-winner, giving the home team a 4-3 win and a berth in the Western Conference Second Round.

OPPOSITE: Duncan Keith celebrates his series-clinching goal late in the third period.
ABOVE TOP: The Blackhawks meet the Predators in the traditional post-series handshake line.
ABOVE BOTTOM: Corey Crawford dons the championship belt teammates gave him after his 13-save performance.

GREAT SCOTT!

by ERIC LEAR, BLACKHAWKS TV REPORTER

As a reporter, I've spent my career searching for great stories. Sometimes you have to dig, and other times the perfect story falls right into your lap. There was no digging done on my part for this one. Scott Darling did all the work.

His journey had an auspicious start. Like most players in the National Hockey League, Darling was a touted young prospect. The Phoenix Coyotes made him the 12th goaltender selected in the sixth round of the 2007 draft, but alcohol and anxiety issues almost derailed his career while he attended the University of Maine. After two seasons with the Black Bears, he was dismissed from the program, and his career started to head even further south, both figuratively and geographically.

With the college hockey hotbed of New England in his rearview mirror, Darling took off for a place known more for Cajun cuisine than skating. He joined up with the Louisiana IceGators of the Southern Professional Hockey League, where his struggles continued. He posted a 6-22 record with a goals-against average just shy of four and wasn't asked back for the following season.

Adversity tends to play a big role in any good story, and Darling dealt with his fair share of it. His story took a positive turn, however, after leaving Louisiana as he regained his focus—and sobriety—and continued his circuitous route to his dream of playing in the NHL.

All in all, Darling played on eight different teams in four leagues over four years after leaving college, and after a stint in the Nashville Predators organization in 2013-14, the Illinois native signed to play hockey in his home state.

Darling was focused on sharpening his game with the Rockford IceHogs when the Blackhawks came calling, and on Oct. 26 he became the first former SPHL player to play in the NHL. Darling stopped 32 of 33 shots, picking up his first career victory and getting First Star of the Game honors. He went on to win five of his first six starts and earned the backup job for good late in the season.

His story would be great if it ended there.

Darling and I had one thing in common when the postseason began: We both planned on having a great view of playoff hockey in our first year with the Blackhawks. His view from the bench would be slightly better than mine from the press box, but we were both there as a part of the organization we grew up watching. However, Darling's view changed in a hurry. Nashville tallied three goals in the first period of Game 1, and he swapped spots with Corey Crawford.

He wasn't tested much early on, which gave him a chance to ease into his first playoff game. He faced just four shots in the second period as the Blackhawks scored three goals to tie the game and quiet the crowd at Bridgestone Arena. As the night went on, Darling's workload increased. He made 15 saves in the third period, including one of the best I've ever seen: Colin Wilson slid a no-look backhand pass to a wide-open Ryan Ellis in front of the net. As the puck left his stick, Predators fans were already out of their seats. Wilson started to raise his arms in celebration. Darling had other plans. He went from post to post to make a pad save that'll be the first clip on his highlight reel for years to come.

Had that puck snuck past his 6-foot-6 frame, the Predators would've taken a 4-3 lead. Instead, Darling stood tall and stopped 17 shots in the first overtime and six in the second. Rather than stumbling out of the gates in the first game of the postseason, Darling helped the Blackhawks complete the thrilling comeback.

Joel Quenneville isn't one to spit out too many superlatives, so it stuck with me when he said during his postgame press conference that Darling's 42-save clinic was one of the best relief performances he'd ever seen. Given the circumstances, it's hard to disagree.

You could call Darling a warrior for battling back from adversity and achieving his dream, but that's a term he reserves for his mother, a two-time cancer survivor. I just call him a Stanley Cup champion. ▥

SECOND ROUND

by EMERALD GAO

If the cauldron of the Stanley Cup Playoffs is where rivalries are forged, it's safe to say that the Blackhawks and the Minnesota Wild have become true antagonists after clashing in the play-offs for three straight years. One might argue that since Chicago has won all three matchups, the relationship is more domination than conflict. After all, this is the official tally so far in the annual reunion of quarreling Midwestern cousins, and you are not listening to a broken record.

2013: Chicago won 4-1 in the conference quarterfinals.

2014: Chicago won 4-2 in the second round.

2015: Chicago won 4-0, again in the second round.

However, at the beginning of May, many thought this could be Minnesota's year to end its run of misery against the Blackhawks. The Wild had just finished ousting division winner St. Louis in six triumphant games, and they were blessed with depth throughout the lineup. Most importantly, their precarious situation in net was finally resolved, as the acquisition of 2015 Vezina Trophy finalist Devan Dubnyk in January proved to be the most valuable in-season deal.

The Blackhawks would have to be at their best to get past a seasoned and vengeful Wild squad, and they came out roaring in Game 1, as Brandon Saad scored on the first shot of the series after victimizing star defense-man Ryan Suter with an outside move. The Blackhawks tacked on two more goals in the first period, but the visitors stormed back with a three-goal flurry of their own in the middle frame. Just when it seemed like the Wild had enough momentum to overpower the Blackhawks, a fluttering shot by rookie Teuvo Teravainen—playing for the first time since Game 2 of the first round—fooled Dubnyk and gave the home side a 4-3 lead that would not be vanquished.

Game 2 began as a much tighter affair, remaining scoreless through the halfway point before Marian Hossa robbed Suter in the neutral zone and fed Jonathan Toews for the opening tally while shorthanded. Patrick Kane added a pair of goals, and Corey Crawford made 30 saves on 31 shots, including several important stops after having his mask broken by a high blast. The win was Chicago's eighth consecutive home playoff victory over Minnesota, and the team headed to the Twin Cities full of confidence.

Every playoff series is different: Some require a true team effort while others are dominated thoroughly by a couple of names. This series belonged to the latter category, showcasing Kane's mesmerizing talents and Crawford's return to form after a shaky Nashville series. The two combined to give the Blackhawks a 1-0 win in Game 3 and a 3-0 stranglehold on the series, as Kane scored in his fourth straight game and Crawford made 30 saves against a visibly frustrated Wild team.

Afterward, Minnesota Head Coach Mike Yeo summarized his team's inability to beat Crawford: "He's a star against us. He's Brodeur, he's Roy, he's everybody. We've got to find a way to solve that."

They had one last chance to do so in Game 4, but as the Blackhawks have done so often lately to so many aggrieved opponents, they finished the series off in style, building a 4-1 lead as Kane extended his goal streak to five games. Crawford held strong with 34 saves, withstanding a late charge from the hosts to emerge with a 4-3 win. Improbably, Kane's post-series comments included the suggestion that "there are some areas that I can try to improve a little bit."

Not much could temper the accomplishment of completing the sweep over a divisional rival, but the long-term loss of defenseman Michal Rozsival to a broken ankle would prove to be a major challenge for Chicago in the next two rounds. III

OPPOSITE: Corey Crawford makes a pad save as Zach Parise crowds the crease.

GAME ONE
MAY 1, 2015
W 4-3

The Blackhawks kicked off their Second Round matchup against Minnesota with a bang, scoring three unanswered goals in the first period, including Brandon Saad's opening goal on the first shot of the series. But the team's 3-0 lead was quickly erased, as Jason Zucker, Zach Parise and Mikael Granlund made it a tie game midway through the second period. Rookie Teuvo Teravainen notched his first career Stanley Cup Playoffs goal and eventual game-winner with a fluttering shot from the boards in the final minute of the middle frame. "I think that wasn't the biggest shot," Teravainen said after the game. "But sometimes good things happen when I shoot."

ABOVE TOP: Marcus Kruger, who scored his first goal of the postseason late in the first period, rushes the puck up ice.
ABOVE BOTTOM: The United Center erupts after the final horn as Chicago takes a 1-0 series lead.

UNDERRATED AND INDISPENSIBLE

by JOHN WIEDEMAN, BLACKHAWKS RADIO PLAY-BY-PLAY ANNOUNCER

Walk the United Center concourse on a Blackhawks game night and you can't avoid bumping into fans wearing Blackhawks sweaters— red, white, black and even green. Toews, Kane, Keith, Seabrook, Crawford, Hossa…the familiar names on the back are too many to count, and for good reason. There are other Blackhawks players who don't get the same recognition, who may not be known for setting up or scoring big goals, but because of their overall reliability, especially in crucial situations, they are equally significant.

Two Swedish-born Blackhawks, Marcus Kruger and Niklas Hjalmarsson, seem to define the term "underrated." To the untrained eye, the little plays that Kruger and Hjalmarsson routinely make to help the Blackhawks win games might go unnoticed. But to those who understand their value, those same little plays are the difference between a win and a loss on many occasions. Their timely contributions have earned the respect of teammates, fans and more in the hockey world.

During the Blackhawks' 2015 Stanley Cup run, Kruger and Hjalmarsson played key roles defensively while supplementing the offensive attack, each in their own way. In Kruger, the Blackhawks have a smart, determined, energetic player who sacrifices for his teammates. He blocks shots, takes hits to protect the puck or make a play, kills penalties, wins critical faceoffs and takes a beating in front of the opposing net and in the dirty areas.

In Hjalmarsson, the Blackhawks have possibly the most undervalued player in the NHL. He rarely makes a bad decision with the puck, absorbs big hits to make a play, blocks key shots (he led the playoffs in this category), puts himself in potentially injurious positions by stepping up at the Blackhawks blue line to disrupt rushes and is undoubtedly one of the best poke-checkers in the game. Offensively, Hjalmarsson doesn't have the dynamic reputation of other defensemen, but he makes simple, sensible plays and has a true knack for getting his point

shots through to the net for tips and deflections.

Kruger centered an effective fourth line with the two Andrews—Desjardins and Shaw—while working to shut down the Predators in the Nashville series as Chicago eventually prevailed 4-2. In the Second Round against Minnesota, Kruger scored his first goal of the playoffs in Game 1, then keyed a defensive effort that helped ensure a four-game sweep.

Hjalmarsson, a left-handed shooter who played the right side opposite Johnny Oduya, frustrated Minnesota repeatedly whenever the Wild began to generate chances. He also made a key play on the game-winning goal in Game 1 when he took a loose puck at center ice and shot it into the Wild zone. As it caromed around the boards to the left wing side, rookie Teuvo Teravainen received it and promptly fired home the winner. Kruger and Hjalmarsson also demonstrated their penalty-killing prowess in all four games against the Wild, who never quite got on track in the series.

In the physical conference final against Anaheim, Kruger took an abundance of hard hits in Games 1 and 2 as the Ducks tried to intimidate the Blackhawks early on. Undaunted, he then took ownership of a distinguished place among all-time Blackhawks players by scoring the game-winning goal in triple overtime of Game 2, ending the longest game in team history to tie up the series.

Meanwhile, Hjalmarsson had to defend against the likes of Ryan Getzlaf and Corey Perry, two of the league's top point producers. Both he and Kruger played key roles in thwarting Anaheim's lethal power play, which up to that point in the playoffs was the league's finest. Moreover, Head Coach Joel Quenneville consistently employed the Kruger-Desjardins-Shaw line to stymie the Ducks' aggressive offense as well as protect leads in the dying minutes of games.

In the 2015 Stanley Cup Final, the potent Tampa Bay Lightning featured an offensive attack that led the playoffs in goals. The Blackhawks' stoppers were up for the

challenge, this time working hard to keep sniper Steven Stamkos goalless. The Lightning also featured a seemingly unstoppable line dubbed "The Triplets," who ripped through opponents on the way to the Final. The trio did register some points against the Blackhawks, but Kruger's line, when called upon, did a commendable job holding them in check.

In the last minutes of the deciding Game 6 at the United Center, Kruger, Hjalmarsson and company ran off crucial seconds as the Lightning played with an empty net and six attackers to try to keep the series alive. Their tenacious defensive play was instrumental in helping the Blackhawks clinch a home-ice championship for the first time in 77 seasons.

When Hjalmarsson and Kruger made their debuts with the Blackhawks back in 2007-08 and 2010-11, respectively, few could have predicted that both would be key players in the team's last two Stanley Cup runs. Hjalmarsson, in fact, is now one of just six Blackhawks to have been part of all three championships.

When Game 6 ended and the unforgettable scene of Lord Stanley's Cup being passed from Blackhawk to Blackhawk unfolded, the two Swedish-born players took their rightful turns. As each raised the Cup before 22,000 fans inside the United Center and millions more watching on TV, Marcus Kruger and Niklas Hjalmarsson must have felt the boundless appreciation of Blackhawks fans in Chicago and around the world. Ⅲ

GAME TWO
MAY 3, 2015
W 4-1

Chicago's big names stepped up in Game 2, which ended 4-1 in the Blackhawks' favor, extending their playoff home win streak over the Wild to eight games dating back to the 2013 championship run. With the game scoreless midway through the second frame, Marian Hossa forced a turnover at the center line while on the penalty kill and served up the puck to Jonathan Toews, who put the Blackhawks on the board with the opening goal; the helper marked Hossa's seventh assist in eight games. Patrick Kane tallied two goals to make it 101 points in 101 career Stanley Cup Playoffs games, Patrick Sharp also found the back of the net, and Corey Crawford stopped 30 of 31 shots by the visitors to contribute to the victory.

OPPOSITE TOP: Corey Crawford stretches out to make one of his 30 saves.
OPPOSITE BOTTOM: Andrew Shaw and teammates get loose by playing sewer ball in the hallway before the game.
ABOVE: The Blackhawks and their fans celebrate Patrick Sharp's third-period goal.

GAME THREE
MAY 5, 2015
W 1-0

After a strong showing in Game 2, Corey Crawford was put to the test in Minnesota and delivered a sensational performance, outdueling the Wild's Devan Dubnyk in a 1-0 win. Highlights in the 30-save effort included an unbelievable point-blank stop on Nino Niederreiter in the second period and a blocker parry to stymie Mikael Granlund on a breakaway. Patrick Kane's first-period power-play goal was the only tally the Blackhawks needed as Crawford earned his fourth career playoff shutout. "It's never easy, especially against this team in their building," he said after the game. "They came hard the whole night, but our guys stood strong. Especially at the end, we were all together as a unit."

OPPOSITE: Corey Crawford makes one of 30 saves in his first shutout of the playoffs.
ABOVE TOP: Patrick Kane's power-play tally in the first period was the difference-maker in Game 3.
ABOVE BOTTOM: Linemates Jonathan Toews, Brandon Saad and Marian Hossa wind down after the game.

GAME FOUR
MAY 7, 2015
W 4-3

Brent Seabrook opened the scoring midway through the first period of Game 4, and Chicago maintained a 4-1 lead with 3:07 remaining in the game, but Minnesota did not go quietly in its desperation to avoid elimination. Jason Pominville and Nino Niederreiter scored 51 seconds apart after Devan Dubnyk was pulled for the extra attacker, setting up a nervewracking ending to the game, but the Blackhawks survived the late rush from the home team. In completing its second-round sweep of the Wild with a 4-3 win, Chicago became the first team to reach the conference finals at least five times in a seven-year span since the Colorado Avalanche (1996-2002).

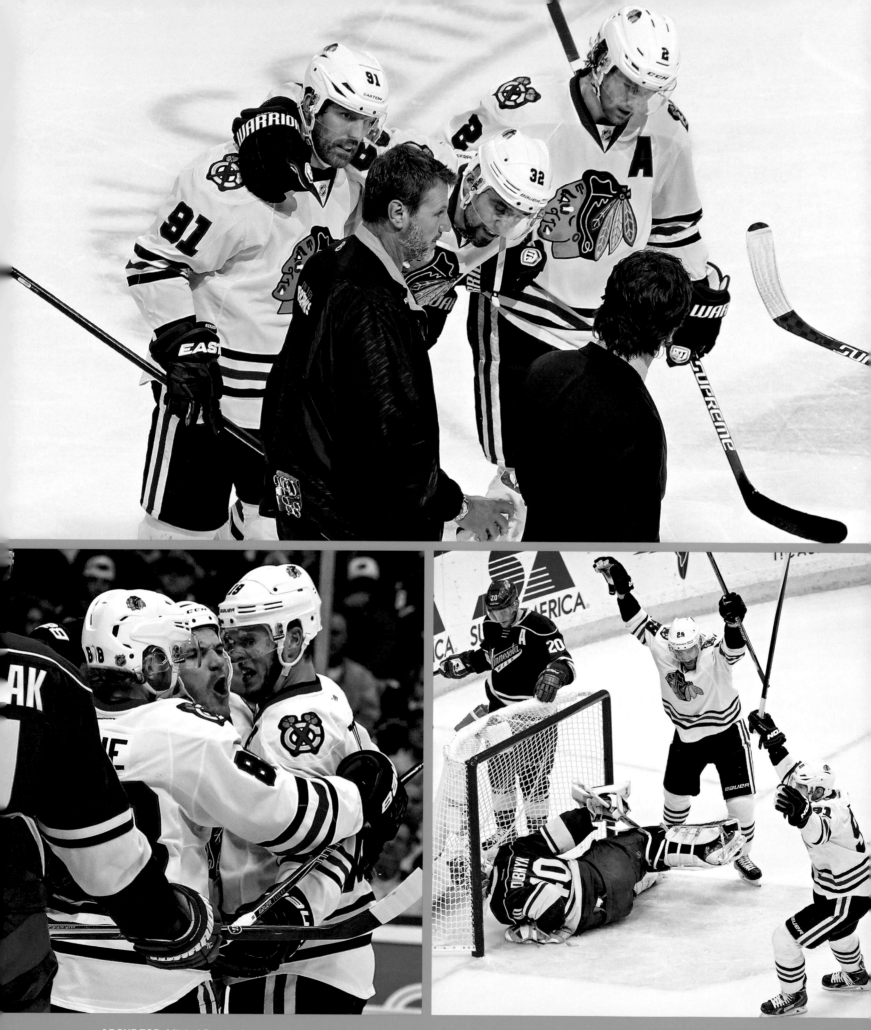

ABOVE TOP: Michal Rozsival is helped off the ice by teammates and staff after suffering an ankle injury.
ABOVE BOTTOM LEFT: Teammates hug Andrew Shaw after his power-play goal.
ABOVE BOTTOM RIGHT: Bryan Bickell and Brad Richards celebrate another goal near the Wild crease.

A GENERATIONAL TALENT

by DENIS SAVARD, BLACKHAWKS AMBASSADOR

as told to Eric Lear

Simply put, we're lucky. Chicago is lucky.

From October to June over the past eight years, we've been blessed to have one of the best players in the league suit up in a Blackhawks sweater. And we're also fortunate to have Patrick Kane around for at least another eight years.

Just look at what he's accomplished before the age of 26: three Stanley Cups, the Calder Trophy, a Conn Smythe—and he could've won league MVP last season had he not gotten hurt. Though I know he's incredibly proud of all those accomplishments, he'd be the first to tell you that the only trophies that matter are the three Stanley Cups. That's one of the many reasons why I admire him so much. He'd rather win the Stanley Cup than individual awards.

When I first saw the 18-year-old Kane at training camp eight years ago, I knew that those individual awards—and hopefully a Stanley Cup or two—were within reach. It was Kane's first camp since being selected as the top overall pick in the 2007 draft, and it was Jonathan Toews' first as well. I was in pretty good company given that it was my first camp as head coach. I could tell right then and

there that we had something special and that the future was bright.

Sometime during camp, I sat down with Patrick to talk about his style of play. It was natural for me to work with him because he plays a similar style of hockey as I did—though he's way better, trust me. Patrick is a natural playmaker with a variety of weapons. He even has a pretty good spin-o-rama, though he did steal it from me because I didn't teach it to him. (I told him he owes me a check every time he does it.)

He's got great hands, speed and vision. In my opinion, Wayne Gretzky had the best vision of all time, but Kane doesn't fall too far behind. When I watch a game and Kane's on the ice, I don't watch him; instead I watch his linemates. That's the best way to see the play develop around him and to really appreciate his otherworldly talent and vision on the ice.

In Game 6 of the Stanley Cup Final, Kane's uncanny vision was on display with the game's first goal. He had the puck just inside the Tampa Bay zone along the right boards. Even though J.T. Brown and Jason Garrison were both closing in and putting pressure on him, he was able to see Duncan Keith rushing up ice. He delivered a perfect saucer pass right on the tape of the eventual Conn Smythe winner's stick, and the Blackhawks were on their way to another Stanley Cup.

Whether it's a key assist like that or scoring the next goal to seal the series, Patrick always plays his best in big moments. It takes a special person to do that. It's hard. I've been there, not at the stage that he's played on so many times, but I know how hard it is to play the type of game he does because the expectations are so high.

He's scored a Cup-clinching goal and series-clinching goals to go along with playoff hat tricks. The repeated postseason success shows he's a generational talent in his prime. So next time you sit down to watch Kane—or his linemates—make sure you truly appreciate how lucky you are to have him on your favorite team. ▥

ABOVE: Denis Savard and Patrick Kane are the only two players in Blackhawks history to reach the 500-point mark in their first seven seasons.

HE'S SCORED A CUP-CLINCHING GOAL AND SERIES-CLINCHING GOALS TO GO ALONG WITH PLAYOFF HAT TRICKS. THE REPEATED POSTSEASON SUCCESS SHOWS HE'S A GENERATIONAL TALENT IN HIS PRIME.

WESTERN CONFERENCE FINAL

by EMERALD GAO

Disneyland may boast year-round attractions, but this past May the most entertaining rollercoaster ride in Anaheim could be found just a few miles down the road, as the Blackhawks commenced an extraordinary series against the Ducks. The Western Conference's top seed had cruised through the first two rounds, sweeping the Winnipeg Jets before dispatching the Calgary Flames in five, and both teams were well-rested, Chicago enjoying nine days in between games and Anaheim getting six.

Ducks goaltender Frederik Andersen was airtight in Game 1, making 16 saves in the first period and 32 of 33 overall to keep Chicago at bay in a 4-1 win for Anaheim. The fun started in Game 2, with the score tied 2-2 going into the third period, then the fourth. Then the fifth.

The two scoreless overtime periods alone warrant an oral history: Anaheim struck iron three times, and in the second overtime, Andrew Shaw head-butted the puck past Andersen, but the goal was dismissed on a technicality despite retaining full style points. So the Blackhawks soldiered on—approaching and then passing the franchise record for longest playoff game—until late in the third overtime, when Marcus Kruger batted the winning goal into the open side of the net.

"As intense a game as I've ever been a part of," was Head Coach Joel Quenneville's summation. "Both teams left it out on the rink."

The Ducks recovered to smother the Blackhawks 2-1 in Game 3, killing off five penalties and displaying their penchant for quick turnarounds, both between and within games. This was certainly true again in Game 4, when Anaheim spotted Chicago a 3-1 lead as late as the third period, but scored three times in 37 seconds—the second-quickest three-goal burst in Stanley Cup Playoffs history—to take a sudden lead and stun the United Center crowd into silence.

It could have been a crushing sequence of events. Instead, the Blackhawks found a level of resilience they weren't accustomed to needing, tying the game before Antoine Vermette completed the thriller in double OT.

"Another team, that would break your backs," Corey Crawford mused, "but we kept playing."

Still, questions began to pile up. Were the Blackhawks tiring themselves out, racking up this many overtime periods? Would the steep incline in ice time take its toll on a defensive group already down a man? To many, it seemed only a matter of time before Anaheim's sledgehammer brand of hockey would grind Chicago into dust.

"No human can withstand that many hits," assured Ryan Kesler after Game 4, but as the Ducks found out, trying to bash the Blackhawks into submission can sometimes feel like punching a waterfall. Contact will be made, sure, but at what expense of energy?

Game 5 seemed to validate Anaheim's approach: Kesler collected seven hits, and Matt Beleskey's winner on the first shift of overtime undid Jonathan Toews' superhuman effort late in regulation to score twice and force overtime for a third time in the series.

Back in Chicago for their first elimination test of the postseason, Quenneville showed the deftness of a Grandmaster moving his king out of check. A few lineup adjustments were made, more attention paid to optimizing matchups, and the result was a comfortable 5-2 victory—iced by a pair of late insurance goals from the fourth line—to force a winner-take-all clash with redemption on the line for both sides after Game 7 exits the previous spring.

Chicago was merciless. Toews picked up where he left off, scoring twice on enemy ice, and the visitors built up a 4-0 lead before the beleaguered Ducks were ready to fight back. Anaheim managed to cut the lead in half, but Brent Seabrook's power-play blast with 6:37 remaining signaled the end for the home side, as the Blackhawks secured a Stanley Cup Final appearance for the third time in six seasons and ensured that there would be no smiles that night in "the happiest place on earth." ▥

OPPOSITE: Andrew Shaw yells after scoring a big insurance goal for the Blackhawks in Game 6 of the Western Conference Final.

GAME ONE
MAY 17, 2015
L 4-1

After a nine-day break between series, the Blackhawks faced off against the Western Conference's top-seeded Anaheim Ducks. The home side took a two-goal lead on goals by Hampus Lindholm and Kyle Palmieri, while Frederik Andersen stopped all 16 shots he faced in the first period, including a stick save on Patrick Kane with a gaping net behind him. Brad Richards tallied a last-minute goal in the second period to cut the lead in half, but the Ducks possessed the puck and limited Chicago's opportunities for the final 20 minutes. Jakob Silfverberg put the puck into an empty net to cap off the 4-1 win for Anaheim.

OPPOSITE: Andrew Shaw gets into a scrum near Ducks goalie Frederik Andersen.
ABOVE TOP: David Rundblad uses his skate to kick the puck away from Kyle Palmieri.
ABOVE BOTTOM: Players lace up in preparation for Game 1.

GAME TWO

MAY 19, 2015

W 3-2 (3OT)

Understatement of the year: It took a long time to decide a victor in Game 2. In fact, the contest required nearly six periods of hockey played over 116 minutes. Marcus Kruger became the sudden-death hero when he capitalized on his own deflection at 16:12 of the third extra period, giving the Blackhawks a 3-2 win over the Ducks and ending the longest game in franchise history. Andrew Shaw opened the scoring in regulation, then used his head in the second overtime when he butted the puck in from close range, but alas, his crafty bid was waved off. Corey Crawford was a force in net, making a career-high 60 saves, and after an intense and hard-fought battle, Chicago evened the series at one game apiece.

OPPOSITE: Marian Hossa and Brad Richards celebrate a first-period goal.
ABOVE TOP: Marcus Kruger bats the puck behind Frederik Anderson for the game-winner in triple overtime.
ABOVE BOTTOM: Kruger faces off against Ryan Getzlaf.

"Some of us thought it was over; some of us thought it was going to be coming back," Blackhawks forward Patrick Sharp said of Andrew Shaw's infamous header in the second overtime period of Game 2. "I'm not sure why that's not allowed. I know it's in the rule book, but that's a pretty athletic play and a pretty entertaining play as well." Added Shaw: "I mean, at that point you react in the moment and try to get it in. I understand [the rule], but I think if anyone can ever pull that off it should still be a goal."

THE LONGEST GAME

by JUDD SIROTT, BLACKHAWKS RADIO STUDIO HOST

It's 11 p.m. Pacific time. Game 2 of the Western Conference Final between the Chicago Blackhawks and Anaheim Ducks—an instant classic—is deep into triple overtime. I've been standing for almost five hours because the visiting booth at Honda Center is more like an undersized broom closet. I haven't eaten since we got to the building at 4 p.m.; luckily, I've got some trail mix buried in my computer bag. And a bathroom break? Good luck. There are only two toilets for the entire press box contingent, which overflowed into the second balcony.

None of that dawned on me as I was watching until the Blackhawks dumped the puck deep in the Ducks zone with 4 minutes left in the sixth period. Andrew Desjardins dug the puck out of the left corner, zipped around the net and fed a pass up to Brent Seabrook at the right point. Seabrook and his defense partner, Johnny Oduya, dished back and forth across the blue line, before Seabrook one-timed a skipping puck on net. Marcus Kruger whacked it home from the top of the crease for the game-winner at 16:12 of triple overtime, giving Chicago a 3-2 victory that evened the series at 1-1 and ending the longest game in Blackhawks franchise history.

Troy Murray, John Wiedeman and I exchange some inspired high-fives, and I reach for my phone to text Rogo—Adam Rogowin, the team's senior director of public relations—a guest request.

"Desjardins please," I type, because I can already see that NBC and Sportsnet have grabbed game-winning collaborators Kruger and Seabrook.

Troy and I start to break down the game and its significance—it was Anaheim's first loss at home in three playoff rounds. Moments later, the affable Desjardins jumps on the postgame show.

"How did the game-winner develop?"

"How did Seabrook, Oduya, Duncan Keith and Niklas Hjalmarsson log all that ice time?" (Each played 46 minutes or more.)

"How important was it to win this game, send the series back to Chicago tied at one and give the Ducks something to think about?"

I text Rogo again because I know Desjardins is gassed: "Last question coming from Troy."

"How are you feeling after playing more than 27 minutes, Andrew?"

Later, Rogo sends me a picture of Desjardins and tells me a great story: "He said, 'I'll do whatever you want, but can I get a chair?'"

Rogowin had hustled down the narrow, dimly lit hallway outside the visiting locker room and swiped a folding chair for the exhausted winger.

Troy and John depart for the team bus. During a quick break, WGN Engineer Krista Flores and I try to figure out how long the postgame show needs to go. It's getting close to 2 a.m. Chicago time; we were supposed to be off the air hours ago.

"I have Kruger if you want it," says the slight, seasoned pro Mike Noto, our booth engineer in Anaheim.

"Let's get to it right after this break. How long do we have, Krista?"

"30 seconds," she says.

Noto had taped the Game 2 hero from the podium. Radio gold.

"I lost sight of the puck when it went D-to-D," said Kruger, who logged 29 minutes and got flattened by Ducks defenseman Clayton Stoner at the start of triple overtime. "I think it hit my glove first, then I just tried to get a stick on it. Happy to put it in."

ABOVE: Andrew Desjardins rests his weary legs in a folding chair during his postgame radio interview.

Andrew Shaw nearly had us out of there a period earlier. Shaw, whose famous shin pads earned the Blackhawks a triple-overtime win during the 2013 Stanley Cup Final against the Boston Bruins, had headed a fluttering rebound behind Ducks goalie Frederik Andersen.

As the players celebrated on the ice, John joined in from the booth, but Troy jumped in.

"Hold on, wait a minute," he said.

Initially called no goal on the ice, the ruling was upheld after review because Shaw deliberately directed the puck into the net with something other than his stick.

Kruger's overtime winner typified the Blackhawks' resilience during a punishing seven-game series against the Ducks and represented one of four sudden-death wins the team notched during the 2015 playoff run.

Incredibly, overtime was never on the table once the Blackhawks advanced to the Stanley Cup Final, despite each of the first five games of that series with the Lightning being decided by only one goal. No team even had more than a one-goal lead in the entire matchup until Patrick Kane gave the Blackhawks a 2-0 edge late in Game 6, making it the tightest championship series in 64 years.

In 2010 and 2013, the Blackhawks needed some overtime magic in the final round to hoist the Cup. They won two of three in sudden death against the Bruins, notching an impressive 5-2 mark in overtime games during their wire-to-wire run to the 2013 championship. Three years earlier, the Blackhawks went 3-1 in extra time, capped by Kane's overtime cup-clincher in Philadelphia, earning the franchise its first Stanley Cup title since 1961.

Kane didn't need to sit down after that goal. And no one was looking at their watch. ▥

GAME THREE
MAY 21, 2015
L 2-1

The Blackhawks had yet to win a game all postseason after outlasting their opponents in multiple overtime periods, and Game 3 at the United Center would prove no different as Chicago was stifled in a 2-1 loss to the Ducks. The Blackhawks' power play was unable to strike on any of their five opportunities, including four in the first 20 minutes. Patrick Maroon opened the scoring for the visitors, but Patrick Kane tallied his first of the series late in the opening period to keep the game even. The Ducks regained the edge with a last-minute goal of their own in the second frame, as Simon Despres netted his first career playoff goal for the eventual game-winner.

OPPOSITE: The Michael Jordan statue, wearing a Blackhawks jersey, welomes fans to the United Center.
ABOVE TOP: Kris Versteeg and Andrew Cogliano fight for the puck.
ABOVE BOTTOM: Mark LaRoque (carrying the Williams family Eagle Feather staff), Lieutenant Junior Grade Gene D. Sweeney and Command Sergeant Major Mark Bowman are honored during pregame as Jim Cornelison performs the national anthem.

GAME FOUR
MAY 23, 2015

W 5-4 (2OT)

Game 4 was yet another United Center marathon, and Antoine Vermette was up for the challenge, providing the game-winner in a frantic, back-and-forth 5-4 win over Anaheim in double overtime. The trade-deadline acquisition put away his own rebound from near the goal line at 5:37 of the second overtime period to help Chicago tie up the Western Conference Final once more. The Ducks erased a 3-1 deficit and took the lead with a three-goal rush in the span of 37 seconds midway through the third period, but Patrick Kane beat Frederik Andersen on the power play shortly after to knot the score and force overtime. With the victory, the Blackhawks improved their 2015 record in overtime contests to 4-0.

ABOVE TOP: Corey Crawford keeps his eye on the puck while under pressure from Anaheim captain Ryan Getzlaf.
ABOVE BOTTOM: The Blackhawks celebrate after evening up their conference final series with the Ducks.

GAME FIVE
MAY 25, 2015
L 5-4 (OT)

The Blackhawks found themselves down 3-0 in the first 15 minutes of Game 5 but returned for the second period with their signature sense of composure. Chicago chipped away at the deficit, getting goals from Teuvo Teravainen and Brent Seabrook in the middle frame, and Jonathan Toews forced overtime with an impressive individual drive, scoring two goals in the final 2 minutes of the game with Corey Crawford pulled. But it was Anaheim's Matt Beleskey who broke through just 45 seconds into overtime, giving his team a 5-4 victory and pushing the Blackhawks to the brink of elimination for the first time all postseason.

OPPOSITE: Bryan Bickell collides with Hampus Lindholm.
ABOVE TOP: Matt Beleskey flies through the air after scoring the game-winner just 45 seconds into sudden death.
ABOVE BOTTOM: Jonathan Toews reacts to the Blackhawks' overtime loss in Anaheim.

GAME SIX
MAY 27, 2015
W 5-2

In the most crucial game of the season to date, Joel Quenneville reunited Patrick Kane and Jonathan Toews on the top line, exercising his so-called "nuclear option." After a scoreless first period, the Blackhawks jumped out to a three-goal lead in the second frame thanks to Brandon Saad, Marian Hossa and Kane, with Duncan Keith recording assists on all three tallies and setting a franchise record for defensemen in the process. Although the Ducks narrowed the deficit with two goals in the third, Andrew Shaw tallied twice late in regulation to ice the Blackhawks' 5-2 win and force a winner-take-all Game 7 in Anaheim.

OPPOSITE: Corey Crawford celebrates at the final horn after making 30 saves in the win.
ABOVE TOP: Andrew Desjardins looks to make a pass from below the goal line against Anaheim's defense.
ABOVE BOTTOM LEFT: Duncan Keith's three second-period assists set a franchise record among defensemen in the playoffs.
ABOVE BOTTOM RIGHT: Fans cheer one of the Blackhawks' five goals that led to another even series.

GAME SEVEN
MAY 30, 2015
W 5-3

With a berth to the Stanley Cup Final on the line, Jonathan Toews stepped up once more in enemy territory. The captain beat Frederik Andersen just 2:23 into the game, then added another tally on the power play midway through the first, putting the Blackhawks ahead 2-0. Goals from Brandon Saad (right) and Marian Hossa made it 4-0 before Ryan Kesler got Anaheim on the board. The Blackhawks survived the third-period onslaught from the Ducks, who outshot the visitors 38-26. A late back-breaker of a goal from defenseman Brent Seabrook provided enough of a cushion for Chicago to win 5-3 and punch a ticket to the championship series for the third time in six seasons.

ABOVE TOP: Frederik Anderson watches as the puck slips into the net courtesy of Brandon Saad.
ABOVE BOTTOM: Jonathan Toews celebrates his second goal in the first period.

ABOVE: Kyle Cumiskey shakes hands with Simon Despres after prevailing 5-3 in Game 7 of the conference final.
OPPOSITE TOP: The Blackhawks celebrate Brent Seabrook's third-period power-play goal that put the game out of reach.
OPPOSITE BOTTOM: After clinching their third Western Conference title in the last six years, the team poses with—but doesn't touch—the Clarence Campbell Bowl.

CAPTAIN EVERYTHING

by **JAMAL MAYERS, BLACKHAWKS COMMUNITY LIAISON**

as told to Eric Lear

Jonathan Toews is a winner. That's all he does. He's shown year after year at every level of hockey that he's a championship-caliber player, and I've been lucky enough to skate alongside him for two titles.

The first came at the 2007 IIHF World Championship in Russia. I was in the middle of my career; Jonathan had just finished his sophomore year at the University of North Dakota and was the only non-NHL player selected to join us on Team Canada. We were pretty loaded with talent—Cam Ward in goal; Shea Weber on defense; Rick Nash, Eric Staal and Shane Doan among the star forwards. Jonathan began the tournament as a bottom-six guy, but by the end of it he was one of our best players.

I got to know Jonathan pretty well over those three or four weeks, and I got a great sense of what a special player and person he was right from the start. At that point, he was contemplating whether he should go back to school or enter the league. There was no doubt in my mind that he was ready to turn pro. (Though given that I was playing for the St. Louis Blues at the time, I probably should've told him to stay in college.)

After we battled against each other for a few years, I was thrilled to join forces with him in Chicago. I only had one fear when I signed with the Blackhawks. With me being in the twilight of my career, I was afraid that this team would be complacent after winning the Cup in 2010, not hungry to get another. I quickly learned that wasn't the case—and would never be the case on a team led by Jonathan Toews.

Along with the core group of guys—Duncan Keith, Brent Seabrook, Corey Crawford, Patrick Kane, Niklas Hjalmarsson and Marian Hossa—he has created a culture of high expectations. They believe they have a chance to win the Stanley Cup every year, and you can feel that when you come to the team.

Jonathan is a great leader for many reasons. He knows when to say something and when not to. He knows when a teammate needs a hug or when they need a kick in the pants. He's got his finger on the pulse of the locker room and fully understands whatever situation his team is in. It's no wonder Tampa Bay Head Coach Jon Cooper called him "Captain Everything" after Game 1 of the Stanley Cup Final.

In no place was that more evident than Game 7 of the Western Conference Final against the Ducks. Toews knew that Anaheim historically had not fared well closing out series. Last year the Ducks were in the same position; they had a 3-2 advantage over Los Angeles, but eventually lost the series on home ice. I believe he went into that game with the idea that establishing a lead early would give Anaheim that here-we-go-again feeling. Toews scored the first two goals of the game in the opening period and willed the team to victory. To me, that's a dominating performance.

I've heard many stories about Mark Messier and his leadership abilities. I think in 10 to 15 years you're going to hear those same types of stories about Toews. I'm not afraid to compare him to Messier or to one of my favorite players as a kid, Steve Yzerman.

I only see one difference: It took Yzerman, a Hall of Famer, a little while to adjust his game and start to take more responsibility defensively; after he did that, his offensive numbers dropped, but he ended up winning Stanley Cups.

Jonathan didn't go through that process. He could easily score 90 points in a season, but you're not going to win Stanley Cups that way. He's always played two-way hockey, and even helped shape Brandon Saad into a two-way star. When your best player is a generational talent with a great work ethic and standout leadership qualities, it's hard not to follow in line.

I've told Jonny that someday there should be a statue of him outside the United Center next to Bobby Hull and Stan Mikita. That's how highly I think of him.

He's already won so much, and at 27 years old, he's not even close to being done. ▥

OPPOSITE: Jonathan Toews is the 11th player in NHL history to captain his team to three Stanley Cups.

THE CONDUCTOR

by BOB VERDI

On a Saturday morning late in the 2014-15 season—March 7, to be exact—Head Coach Joel Quenneville convened practice at the United Center. The previous night, after two ragged periods, his Blackhawks rescued a 2-1 shootout victory over the Edmonton Oilers. Next up was a visit from the rampaging New York Rangers.

As soon as he took the ice, it was apparent that Coach Q did not plan on taking his whistle for a leisurely skate.

"Let's get ------ off around here!" he bellowed, loud enough to merit a banner headline in Sunday's Daily Herald: "Enough is enough. Quenneville's had it with Hawks' spate of lackluster efforts."

Witnesses reported that players not only listened attentively to his words, as in the famous E. F. Hutton commercial, but conducted rather crisp drills. With only 17 games remaining in the regular season, Quenneville sought to convey a sense of urgency. When the pucks were put away, he brought out a notecard with talking points.

Given the paucity of recorded public outbursts, Coach Q's display was news. It is also noteworthy that Quenneville, a future Hall of Famer with virtually total recall on all matters pertaining to hockey, is strapped for details on his out-of-body experience.

"I honestly don't remember that," said Quenneville, smiling now. "I vaguely remember being angry about something around that time, but that exact moment? What was that date again?"

As for June 15—a Monday night, to be exact—no problem. With 22,424 providing the soundtrack of a constant din, Quenneville's Blackhawks eliminated the Tampa Bay Lightning at the "Madhouse on Madison" in Game 6 of a scintillating Stanley Cup Final. He decided that, considering all the bumps and bruises along the way, this third National Hockey League championship in six years had been the toughest yet.

"But nothing these guys do surprises me," Coach Q concluded. "Unbelievable."

On the surface, that might qualify as a contradiction. After all, if nothing his players accomplish shocks him, then they are routinely, predictably the goods. But Quenneville's message during the celebration was as clear as the one he grumpily delivered at that bygone gathering in March. When it counts, count on the Blackhawks. They are special, and he is honored to be where he is.

"This is really crazy now," Quenneville said. "I mean, it was big in 2010 when we won. And it was a lot bigger in 2013. But now it's gone to another level. The way these amazing fans love this team in Chicago. The way fans love this team everywhere we go. In the States, in Canada.

"It's so tough to win. It's so tough to make the playoffs. Look at our division. Five teams made the playoffs, all seven over .500. The last-place team in our division, Colorado, had 90 points! Then the postseason. We lost in the worst way possible last year—overtime at home in Game 7. That might have helped the appetite this year. We didn't want to go through that again. Hell no.

"Then we fall behind to Anaheim three games to two. It doesn't look good. Triple overtimes, three flights to the West Coast, landing at O'Hare at 3 or 4 in the morning. Are we doing this all for nothing again? But the guys found a way, because they always seem to find a way. I think fans appreciate how hard it is. I know I do."

Fans, even those who happen to be in the Hall of Fame, also appreciate how the Blackhawks play.

"It starts with the coach," said Tony Esposito, a Blackhawks ambassador. "Some coaches want to win every game 1-0. They can put you to sleep. Quenneville has great players, and he lets them play. Speed, skill. They're the most exciting team in the most exciting sport, and he's the man behind it."

What is the genesis of all this? We introduce you to Gerry Cheevers, a Hall of Fame goalie who won two Stanley Cups with the Boston Bruins in the 1970s and is a fellow aficionado of Quenneville's favorite publication, The Racing Form.

OPPOSITE: Joel Quenneville's 73 playoff wins rank first in franchise history among bench bosses.

"WATCHING HIM COACH, IT'S AN EDUCATION," SAID ASSISTANT COACH KEVIN DINEEN. "HE IS A HOCKEY SAVANT. IT'S ALMOST SCARY. MISSES NOTHING ON THE ICE. HAS THE COMPLETE PULSE OF THE TEAM."

"I was broadcasting in Hartford after I retired," said "Cheesey." "Joel was playing with the Whalers. I told him he should go into coaching. Now he's a better coach than he ever was a player. But I didn't know that he would become a freaking genius behind the bench."

Quenneville has secured more titles than any coach or manager in Chicago history except George Halas of the Bears and Phil Jackson of the Bulls. During his tenure with the Blackhawks, Quenneville has climbed to third place for regular-season victories on the all-time list of NHL coaches behind only Scotty Bowman and Al Arbour. Despite his iconic profile, Quenneville is commercial-free. He endorses nothing except winning. Moreover, he has earned three Stanley Cups with three different rosters and three different staffs. Kevin Dineen and Jimmy Waite joined Mike Kitchen as assistants last year. And the beat goes on.

"I played with Joel, and even then he had goals," Dineen said. "He got his broker's license (to sell securities) when he was still active. But watching him coach, it's an education. He is a hockey savant. It's almost scary. Misses nothing on the ice. Has the complete pulse of the team."

After games, Matt Meacham, the Blackhawks' extraordinary video coach, supplies tapes of recent events for instant replays and critiques.

"I can go over to Joel on the plane and mention a certain play," Kitchen said. "I know that even if he hasn't watched what I've watched yet, he will cite exactly what I'm talking about, what happened and when it happened. A photographic memory."

Waite, who did a splendid job with goalies Corey Crawford and Scott Darling, cuts to the essence of Quenneville's reign.

"He is very demanding," Waite said. "But along with that, everybody is accountable. That is a huge part of what this team is about. Do it right, and do it now. Is it fun, though? It's lots of fun. Winning it all is fun, but getting there is also fun."

The coaches are inseparable on the road, though they might see each other more than they see their wives. As the weather warmed during the grueling postseason run, it was commonplace for Quenneville, Kitchen, Dineen, Waite and Meacham to locate an outdoor space beside their hotel after dinner to enjoy cigars and a bottle of wine.

They know how to laugh, and they know how to relax.

"We try to get Joel to pay," Kitchen cracked. "Actually, in all honesty, it's hard to get a check away from Joel."

Until this past summer's massive United Center renovation, Quenneville occupied a tiny, windowless office—hardly reflective of coaching royalty. But he does not preside over an imperial administration. Assistants have their in-game specialties: Kitchen, the defense and penalty kill; Dineen, the power play. Quenneville handles the forwards. Unlike with some staffs, however, the suggestion box is always open.

"We all talk about everything," Dineen said. "Of course, we know who has the final vote. How often does Joel use the hammer? Rarely."

"Joel is a perfectionist, but not really all that hands-on," Kitchen added. "The guys love that, and so do we. He doesn't want us sitting there nodding in agreement to everything he does or says. We challenge him if we have a strong opinion. But if it involves a particular incident, you'd better have your facts ready. And he has a great quality for a head coach: He is unpredictable."

In a locker room he tours sparingly, Quenneville commands and expresses respect. He never throws players under the bus; they are aware of who is driving the bus. More than one has voiced regret about being unable to face him on the bench, because Coach Q owns a wide array of spirited histrionics that officials see rather distinctly. Players, however, can hear Quenneville loud and clear, particularly when he tosses out his go-to epithet. (Someone offered that nobody uses that particular word with quite the same gusto Q does.)

"I am a players' coach," Quenneville said. "I think they appreciate that I don't go around screaming and yelling. I think they like that we have relatively short practices, that I don't call practice just to call practice. And I know they like time to rest, stay fresh. Sometimes you gotta get away from the rink."

Indeed, the Blackhawks get more days off than a college professor. It's about trust. Quenneville let them be between Games 1 and 2 of the Final in Tampa. Their hotel was not far from the beach. But on a shiny afternoon, Brad Richards, who had played there, borrowed wheels to take Jonathan Toews and a couple other teammates to a place that makes juice. A supply of greenish health liquids, heavy on spinach, was on their flight from Chicago. It was already exhausted, so the Blackhawks went searching for spinach juice.

In Florida.

On a day off.

With the beach right over there.

And the pool a slapshot away.

"Very dedicated and responsible group," Q praised. "When I played, we didn't go looking for health juice."

As for the Blackhawks' ineluctable up-tempo style, that is part of the indelible Quenneville brand.

"I've always coached that way," he said. "We are not referees about our system. We don't wear them out with film sessions. We're not cops, telling guys you have to be in this exact quadrant of the ice, so many feet from wherever, you must be right there and no place else.

"We do have a rhyme and reason when we don't have the puck. But when we do have the puck—and we like to think of ourselves as a puck-possession team—it's 'Let's go. Create something.'"

Kitchen corroborates Quenneville's approach.

"I would say that Joel is more rigid about what players are supposed to do in our end than elsewhere on the ice," he said. "But you don't tell a Patrick Kane what to do with the puck when he has it at the other end."

OK, Coach Quenneville, what about this allegation that you don't like young players?

"Oh, that is so untrue, such B.S.," he said, getting his dander up now. "When Brandon Saad came to us a couple years ago, did we use him? Did he play big minutes on top lines? When Trevor van Riemsdyk showed up at training camp last year, was he still young? I didn't know who he was. I didn't know where he came from. I didn't know how to spell his name. Did he earn a place on our roster? Did Teuvo Teravainen play big minutes during the playoffs? Is Scott Darling an old guy? I don't know where that stuff gets started.

"As a coach, you have one kind of leverage. How many minutes does a guy play, and what kind of minutes, in what situations? I don't care how much money a guy makes, what age he is, what country he comes from, what language he speaks or who his agent is. Just play. And play hard. Period."

At the trade deadline in March, the Blackhawks acquired the premier available forward in Antoine Vermette. He scored just one shootout goal in 19 regular-season contests and was a healthy scratch for the first two playoff games in Nashville. Coach?

"It took awhile for him to transition," Quenneville said. "Same with Kimmo Timonen, although he hadn't been playing at all. Goes back to minutes. They both wanted more minutes. I understand that. Vermette winds up playing great in the postseason. I tip my hat to him. He could have gone away and hid. He could have pouted, although that would have been tough in our locker room with our leadership group. But he was very professional about the whole thing. Did I tear him down to build him back up? I take absolutely no credit for how he came through it."

Quenneville's line machinations are a source of wonderment to not only observers, but his assistants. Again, they often partake in decisions—in games, during intermissions or between games—but as Waite commended, "The worst thing you can do when things aren't working is to do nothing, and Joel never just sits back and waits. He processes what he's seeing and reacts."

Denis Savard, the Hall of Fame ambassador whom Quenneville succeeded as head coach just four games into the 2008-09 schedule, is an unabashed admirer.

OPPOSITE: Coach Q gets sprayed with bubbly following Chicago's Game 6 win that capped off his third Stanley Cup title.

"Sometimes I scratch my head at what Joel does with his lines," Savard said. "But tell me, how many times has he screwed up? I'm already on record admitting that I could never coach the way he coaches. If our main guys weren't going on any given night, I would just hope that they got going as the game went on. Joel doesn't operate like that, and the way he puts guys in different situations, on different lines, it's incredible.

"And let me tell you something about Game 7 in Anaheim. Duncan Keith was our most valuable player in the postseason, hands down. I would put Corey Crawford a close second. But the way Q ran that bench in Anaheim *when he didn't even have the last change*, it was crazy good. He had his top guys on when he wanted them, Tazer scores two quick goals, we go up 4-0, and the Ducks are done. Toast. Coach Q was the MVP that game. Like he was conducting an orchestra."

Only James Bond closes a deal like the Blackhawks. In 117 playoff games since Quenneville took over, they are 30-30 over the front part of a series, but a ridiculous 43-14 from Games 4 through 7. Even in series they have lost, they finish strong. Witness the 2011 Western Conference Quarterfinals against the Vancouver Canucks, who won the first three games, then hung on before winning Game 7 in overtime. In the fateful 2014 Western Conference Final against the Los Angeles Kings, the Blackhawks rallied from being down 3-1 in the series to force a Game 7 and lost on a freakish overtime carom that nobody around Chicago likes to discuss. The Blackhawks have played 20 playoff series under Quenneville and won 16.

Kitchen, without revealing any state secrets, points to "adjustments" and how "our guys buy into them." In Game 3 of the Final at the United Center, Tampa Bay defenseman Victor Hedman threaded a masterful 100-foot pass to Ryan Callahan for the Lightning's first goal in a 3-2 victory. Tampa Bay espouses pressure and possession, like the Blackhawks. "They were rink-widing us to death," recalled Kitchen, referring to long stretch

ABOVE: Joel Quenneville shares a tight bond with his coaching staff, including assistants Kevin Dineen and Mike Kitchen.

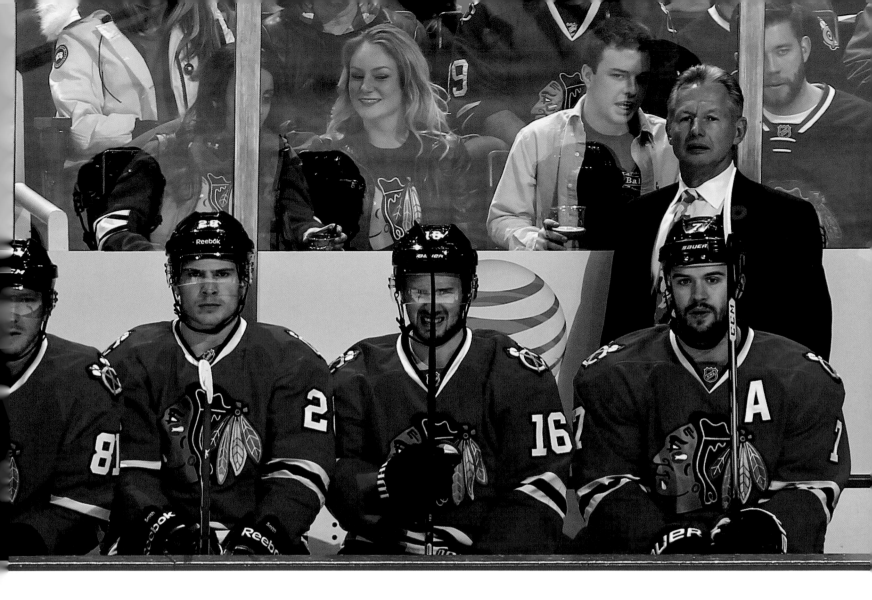

passes to the far blue line and board-to-board exchanges in the neutral zone. Coach Q and staff altered the coverage. The Blackhawks did not lose another game.

"Our guys, their record for finishing, it's like dreaming in color," Quenneville said. "They have a lot of experience, they're poised, and they have that ability to figure out what they're up against. It's amazing, and it requires a certain hockey intelligence, a hockey IQ. But again, I take absolutely no credit for the way, time after time, our guys come through in tough situations. That Anaheim series, it was epic. Tampa Bay, close, every bounce mattered. But the guys got it done."

On March 29, about three weeks after Quenneville's call to arms at practice, the Blackhawks won 4-3 at Winnipeg on Toews' tip-in with 31 seconds left. Coach Q called it the "most important victory" of the season. One night later, the Blackhawks squelched the desperate Kings 4-1 with a superlative effort at the United Center.

There was a special guest that evening. Chairman Rocky Wirtz and wife, Marilyn, love beagles. So they invited Miss P, "Best in Show" winner at the annual Westminster Kennel Club dog show in New York. The handsome beagle got the red carpet treatment, then sat on the glass in the arms of handler William Alexander.

"This will tell you how focused Joel is," Dineen recounted. "After the game, we were talking about how we played. I mentioned to Joel, 'And how about that dog sitting right beside our bench?' After all, it isn't often that you see a dog watching a hockey game. He had no idea what I was talking about. He looked at me like I was nuts."

Quenneville can no more provide details about Miss P than he can about that Saturday morning in March when he vaguely remembers being angry.

"I remember Kevin saying there was a dog at the game," Coach Q concluded. "But I never saw it. Our family, Boo and our three kids, we have two dogs. Miggy and Zarley. Dogs are nice. But I never saw a dog that night. We won a huge game, though. I saw that." ▥

WINNING AT HOME

CHAPTER FOUR

TALENT, POISE AND EXPERIENCE

by BOB VERDI *with* SCOTTY BOWMAN

Scotty Bowman, the Blackhawks' Hall of Fame senior advisor to hockey operations, has earned 14 Stanley Cup championship rings and counting. Beyond that, he knows both 2015 Stanley Cup Final teams like a book. Here, the oracle of hockey shares his knowledge.

Did last June's Final between the Blackhawks and Tampa Bay Lightning meet your expectations?

Naturally, I like the way it ended. But overall, yes, it was good for hockey. Two skilled teams, playing fast. And until Patrick Kane scored the second goal in Game 6, there was never more than a one-goal separation in the entire series. You can't get much tighter than that.

Besides seeing a lot of Blackhawk games, you have a winter residence in Florida and regularly attend Lightning games. Did anything surprise you about the series?

Tampa Bay had the highest-scoring team in the National Hockey League, but they managed only 10 goals in six games and two in the last three. I thought they might score more. That said, it's still about defense and goaltending in the Final. Believe me, I know.

Indeed, you were on the losing end in only four Finals, but three were as coach of the St. Louis Blues in an expansion division wherein one of six new teams qualified for the Final by decree.

Yes, the only established team that I lost with was Detroit in 1995. We had just played a series against Chicago that took something out of us. The Blackhawks were more physical than we anticipated. Only five games but three overtimes. Then in the Final, New Jersey was tight-checking with excellent goaltending and defense, and we got swept. Chicago had the same and basically shut down the Lightning. No team did that to Tampa all year, regular season or playoffs.

You started your NHL coaching career with a pretty good goaltender, didn't you?

You bet. Glenn Hall. He won a Stanley Cup with the Blackhawks in 1961, but by 1967, they were convinced he was going to retire. So they left him unprotected in the expansion draft. We took him in St. Louis, and he wound up playing for us. And he played great. He put us on the map and was terrific in the locker room around the younger players. The Blues got swept their first three years in the Final: by Montreal—twice—and Boston. But in the 1968 Final against the Canadiens, he won the Conn Smythe Trophy as most valuable player even though we lost four straight. They were all one-goal games.

You also won two of your Stanley Cups in the old Stadium.

With Montreal in 1973, in Game 6. That was the year after Bobby Hull left the Blackhawks, but they played really well without him and surprised a lot of people by making it to the Final. Then in 1992, after I took over for Bob Johnson in Pittsburgh, we beat the Blackhawks in four straight. That was the Penguins' second Cup in a row. They were loaded. But so was Chicago. They came into the Final with 11 straight playoff wins and had us on the ropes in Game 1 before we came back to win 5-4.

In the 2015 Final, who impressed you for the Blackhawks?

Start with the goalie, Corey Crawford. He stole the first game in Tampa. They were all over us; then we scored two goals in two minutes late in the third period and won. Crawford does that time after time. The clincher in Boston in 2013 when the Blackhawks won it with two goals in 17 seconds in Game 6—that could have been 4-0 or 5-0 early for the Bruins, except for Crawford.

Why doesn't Crawford receive more acclaim?

Maybe because there are so many stars on the team, the goalie gets overlooked. But his players believe in him, he makes big saves at big times, and doesn't let a bad goal here and there bother him. It took Corey five years in the minors to make it to the NHL. So he didn't come to Chicago with much fanfare. But he's a winner.

And the defense?

Terrific. A lot of people thought our top four guys might run out of gas with all the minutes they played, but they

OPPOSITE: Niklas Hjalmarsson and Brent Seabrook embrace after time expires in Game 6 of the Stanley Cup Final.

"I THOUGHT TAMPA BAY MIGHT SCORE MORE. THAT SAID, IT'S STILL ABOUT DEFENSE AND GOALTENDING IN THE FINAL. BELIEVE ME, I KNOW."

were great. Duncan Keith was fabulous, the best player in the series. Brent Seabrook is always steady. Johnny Oduya played really well, and Niklas Hjalmarsson—he's a warrior. Playing the off side, a left shot on the right, might actually help him defensively even if it restricts him a bit offensively. Nobody ever gets around him. He's the shutdown guy out there against the other team's best, and all those shots he blocks. Remember when Swedish guys were supposed to be soft? Not if you watch him.

Steven Stamkos, their most explosive player, never scored. Surprised about that?

Yes, but it's not like he didn't have chances. Chicago did hold them down, but it wasn't really an airtight series. Both teams had chances, including Stamkos in the last game. Maybe he was pressing. He's a great sniper, though.

Did depth determine the series outcome?

Probably. To be honest, their goalie, Ben Bishop, was hurting. So was Nikita Kucherov, and Tyler Johnson couldn't take faceoffs. Oduya and Andrew Shaw played hurt for Chicago. But look at Shaw, Marcus Kruger and Andrew Desjardins. They were on the ice at crucial times, late in games, last shift or two. The coaches showed a lot of confidence in them, trusted them, and they were terrific.

The Blackhawks have exhibited a knack for closing out series. Any theories?

Amazing. Their three Cups all were in six games. They rarely play a Game 7 in any series. And when they do, like against Anaheim, they finish with two straight wins, clinching on the road. It's a wonderful trait. Probably a combination of talent, poise and experience.

As the all-time leader in coaching victories, what's your take on Joel Quenneville?

He's got the right players on the ice all the time. He lets his players play, but if they're not going on a particular night, he makes changes right away. And his players

like to play for him, especially his best players, which you have to have as a coach. Joel runs the team, he doesn't fool around, but his players have input. He listens. It's a very stable environment.

Tampa Bay wants to follow the Blackhawks' blueprint. See any similarities with the two franchises?

In Chicago, you have a great owner in Rocky Wirtz, who's turned the entire organization around. The product, the priorities. Hiring all sorts of scouts, building a farm system. Tampa Bay has an owner, Jeff Vinik, who's like Rocky. They love him. He's invested in the team, the building and the community. You don't see that often. Two markets where the owners are so popular.

Proud of your son, Stan?

He's got a big job, general manager of an Original Six team in a salary cap era. He's had to let go of some players, but he's made good decisions and spent money in the right places. And, again, he's got the backing. The Blackhawks got cap relief when Kane went down during the season, and Stan got the green light to trade for Antoine Vermette, who came up big.

If you're starting a team in the NHL, is Jonathan Toews your first pick?

I would say so. He has no weaknesses. He's got the ability, the demeanor, always says the right thing, never takes a night off, never takes a shift off. We had Steve Yzerman in Detroit. Same type of guy. Great substance. Jonathan is a leader, and he became captain around guys like Keith and Seabrook, who were there before him. But Jonathan has earned their respect, and he relies on his cabinet, which includes the veterans like Keith and Seabrook, who are also really solid people. Jonathan gives you everything you could want and has everything you could ask for. When Joel says it helps to have No. 19 in the room, that says a lot. ▥

OPPOSITE TOP: Despite suffering back spasms on the morning of Game 6, Andrew Shaw helped the Blackhawks win the Cup.
OPPOSITE BOTTOM: With 45 playoff wins under his belt, Corey Crawford is now tied with Tony Esposito for the franchise record.

GAME ONE
JUNE 3, 2015
W 2-1

After three days of rest, the Blackhawks began the final leg of their Stanley Cup journey with a 2-1 come-from-behind win in Tampa. The Lightning put forth a stifling effort in their own barn, taking an early lead on Alex Killorn's tip-in and holding Chicago to just 13 shots through two periods. But in the third, Corey Crawford denied Ryan Callahan on a breakaway, the first of several plays that reversed the Blackhawks' fortunes. With under 7 minutes to go in regulation, Teuvo Teravainen beat Ben Bishop with a shot from the slot. The youngster wasn't done. Two minutes later he stole the puck from Tampa's Andrej Sustr and tapped it to linemate Antoine Vermette, who netted the game-winner. "Finnish cold," indeed.

OPPOSITE TOP: Patrick Sharp laces up a skate prior to Game 1.
OPPOSITE BOTTOM: Blackhawks fans gather at the glass during warmups.
ABOVE TOP: Duncan Keith congratulates Teuvo Teravainen after his game-tying goal in the third period.
ABOVE BOTTOM: Antoine Vermette fist-pumps after netting one of his three game-winners during the playoffs.

GAME TWO
JUNE 6, 2015
L 4-3

The Bolts tied the series with a 4-3 win in Game 2, but it wasn't easy. Cedric Paquette gave Tampa Bay the lead in the first period, and the second period was chaos, as Andrew Shaw and Teuvo Teravainen bent the score back in Chicago's favor, only to be matched by Tampa Bay's "Triplets" line with two tallies of their own. Brent Seabrook cashed in early in the third off a nifty pass from Jonathan Toews, but a power-play blast by Jason Garrison shortly thereafter gave the Lightning the lead for good. The score wasn't the only thing fluctuating throughout the night: Tampa Bay goaltender Ben Bishop was in and out of the game for then-mysterious reasons, and 20-year-old backup Andrei Vasilevskiy eventually got the win after a 9-minute relief appearance.

OPPOSITE TOP: Corey Crawford leads the team out onto the ice for Game 2.
OPPOSITE BOTTOM: Amalie Arena is lit up for the pregame presentation.
ABOVE: Niklas Hjalmarsson and Duncan Keith defend against Nikita Kucherov, part of Tampa's "Triplets" line.

SWEET HOME CHICAGO

by EDDIE OLCZYK, BLACKHAWKS TV COLOR ANALYST

as told to Eric Lear

Over the past eight seasons, Chicago's hockey RENAISSANCE has been amazing to watch, and I use all capital letters there because it's been that impressive.

Growing up in Niles as a hockey player, I always wondered what it would be like if the Blackhawks, my favorite team, were ever to win a Stanley Cup, and now I've seen it happen three times. This franchise's resurgence and success has galvanized the city from one end of town to the other, and it's really come a long way in a short period of time. Ten years ago, this was not a destination for players. It is now, and that's a credit to Rocky, John, Jay, Stan, Coach Q and his staff.

I've seen the resurgence firsthand in a lot of ways. Everywhere you turned during the Stanley Cup Final you saw banners in streets. You saw the car flags. You saw people wearing the jerseys and the T-shirts and the hats, and there were posters and signs throughout the city.

I think it really struck me as I was driving in for a game late in the postseason. I flipped through five or six radio stations, starting with WGN, and they were all talking about the Blackhawks. That never happened before, but when you're going for your third championship in six seasons and you're the hottest team in town, you have to talk about it. In a city like this, with so much going on, it's pretty special.

Not only is it special, it's also infectious. When you see a winning brand of hockey and you have a lot of great young players, people want to be a part of it. That's why you see the Blackhawks logo all over town and why there's a waiting list to buy season tickets. The Blackhawks' success on the ice has led to an increase in participation in hockey across the city and its suburbs. You can't get ice time anymore because people of all ages—both men and women—are playing the game of hockey.

I think the greatest impact is at the youth level. Kids are seeing the excitement surrounding the Blackhawks and deciding they want to play, and when they do get out on the ice they're wearing Blackhawks sweaters. For me, a Chicago guy and somebody who takes great pride in youth hockey in the state and in our city, that's important because we want to get as many young people—both boys and girls—playing this game as quickly as possible.

We've always had great hockey players here. Now we just have a lot more of them, and I think that's a direct result of how hockey has come a long way in Illinois. Because of the impact this team has had locally, we'll see more and more kids be able to play the greatest game in the world. It reminds me of the impact that Mario Lemieux's Penguins had in the state of Pennsylvania during the '80s and '90s.

I asked myself last year: Who will be the first Chicago kid to get his name on the Stanley Cup for his hometown team? The answer ended up being Scott Darling, who came out of nowhere and did an incredible job for the Blackhawks in the regular season and then in the First Round against Nashville. Now I wonder who will be the second or third? Hopefully in 20 years we'll be talking about the 10th or 15th, and the Blackhawks will have played a huge role in that.

I was one of those kids. I grew up dreaming about playing for my hometown team, and I was lucky enough to be able to do that, but fell short of winning the Cup in my home state. I played my first game as a Blackhawk, I played my 1,000th game as a Blackhawk, and I played my last game as a Blackhawk in 2000. Now I've been lucky enough to witness this RENAISSANCE as an observer out in the community and as a broadcaster alongside my partner, the great Pat Foley. I can't wait to see where it goes from here III

GAME THREE
JUNE 8, 2015
L 3-2

The start of Game 3 came as no surprise, as Tampa Bay opened the scoring for the third time in the series, but Chicago bounced back when Marian Hossa set up Brad Richards on the power play to knot the score at 1-1 through 20 minutes. Brandon Saad found the net early in the third, only for Ondrej Palat to tie the game during a goal-mouth scramble just 13 seconds later. Cedric Paquette capped off an end-to-end rush from defensive standout Victor Hedman late in regulation, giving the visitors a 3-2 win. After Game 2's goalie carousel, Ben Bishop was back in net for the Lightning and proved to be the edge, frustrating the Blackhawks with a 36-save performance.

OPPOSITE TOP: Marian Hossa gets a shot off despite Braydon Coburn's best efforts.
OPPOSITE BOTTOM: Jonathan Toews faces off against Brian Boyle.
ABOVE TOP: Brad Richards celebrates his first-period goal against his former team.
ABOVE BOTTOM: Corey Crawford concentrates as a shot approaches.

GAME FOUR
JUNE 10, 2015
W 2-1

The Blackhawks arrived at the United Center for Game 4 not knowing which goalie they would face. In the end, Andrei Vasilevskiy was tapped to make his first start of the series, but the 20-year-old was outdueled by Corey Crawford, who made 24 saves in Chicago's 2-1 win. Jonathan Toews opened the scoring at 6:40 of the second period, only to be answered by Alex Killorn's tying goal minutes later. Brandon Saad provided the game-winner in the third with a power move to the net. The Bolts pressed for an equalizer, but Crawford and the Blackhawks defense—which combined for 15 blocked shots in the contest—held on for the victory, and the series was even once again.

OPPOSITE: Actor Vince Vaughn (left) and Rage Against the Machine guitarist Tom Morello cheer on the Blackhawks.
ABOVE TOP: Brandon Saad and Brad Richards celebrate Saad's game-winner in the third period.
ABOVE BOTTOM LEFT: Fans brave heavy rain on their way to the United Center.
ABOVE BOTTOM RIGHT: Patrick Sharp and Marian Hossa embrace Jonathan Toews after his 10th goal of the playoffs.

ABOVE: Corey Crawford stops Steven Stamkos, who was held scoreless during the Final.
OPPOSITE: Jonathan Toews sends the puck behind Ondrej Palat and Andrei Vasilevskiy.

GAME FIVE

JUNE 13, 2015

W 2-1

The Blackhawks rode another hot goaltending performance by Corey Crawford—31 saves on 32 shots—en route to a 2-1 Game 5 win. Early in the first period, miscommunication between Lightning netminder Ben Bishop and defenseman Victor Hedman ended in a heavy collision, allowing Patrick Sharp to skate the puck into the net for an early lead. Valtteri Filppula tied the game for Tampa Bay midway through the second period, and 2 minutes into the third period, Kris Versteeg found Antoine Vermette for his fourth goal of the playoffs and second game-winner of the Final. Crawford stopped 15 shots in the last frame to collect the win and give the Blackhawks a chance to clinch the Stanley Cup on home ice for the first time since 1938.

OPPOSITE TOP: Brandon Saad checks Valtteri Filppula into the boards.
OPPOSITE BOTTOM: Players watch as a puck sails behind Ben Bishop's net.
ABOVE TOP: Patrick Sharp puts the puck into an empty net after a collision took out Bishop.
ABOVE BOTTOM: Teuvo Teravainen and Antoine Vermette hug after connecting for the game-winner.

GAME SIX

JUNE 15, 2015

W 2-0

Amidst a torrential downpour that left many fans sopping wet but no less raucous, the Blackhawks shut out the Lightning 2-0—Corey Crawford made 25 saves—to clinch their third Stanley Cup in the last six seasons. The two teams remained scoreless until late in the second period, when Patrick Kane found Duncan Keith streaking into the offensive zone. Keith put his own rebound past Ben Bishop, cementing his case for the Conn Smythe Trophy as playoff MVP. Kane's insurance tally in the third ignited the Blackhawks faithful, who remained on their feet and counted down the last 3 seconds to mark the historical occasion of the team's first home championship in 77 years, then stayed well after the final horn to applaud each player as he took a lap around the ice with Lord Stanley's chalice.

ABOVE TOP: The American flag is projected onto the United Center ice pregame.
ABOVE BOTTOM: Corey Crawford stones Steven Stamkos on a breakaway early in the second period to keep the game scoreless.
OPPOSITE TOP: Duncan Keith lets out a roar after opening the scoring.
OPPOSITE BOTTOM: Patrick Kane smiles after his goal with 5:14 left in regulation.

OPPOSITE: Sans equipment, the Blackhawks celebrate their third Stanley Cup victory in the last six seasons.
ABOVE TOP: Jonathan Toews leaps onto Corey Crawford while Marian Mossa and Niklas Hjalmarsson rejoice at the final horn.
ABOVE BOTTOM: Fans celebrate behind the glass as the Blackhawks gather for a group hug.

SAVING HIS BEST FOR LAST

by JUDD SIROTT, BLACKHAWKS RADIO STUDIO HOST

Ten goals in six games. That's all Blackhawks goaltender Corey Crawford allowed the Tampa Bay Lightning—the most prolific offensive team in the league—during the Stanley Cup Final.

The numbers, however impressive, barely tell the story though. Crawford's path to a second Cup title had the arc of every classic tale.

It started with an eye-catching introduction. The Lightning came out flying at home in Game 1. How much did the Blackhawks have left in the tank after a bruising seven-game series against the Anaheim Ducks?

Crawford kept it close. Trailing 1-0 with just over 8 minutes left, the netminder made his best save of the night, stoning Ryan Callahan on a clean breakaway.

Two minutes later, Teuvo Teravainen tied it, then set up Antoine Vermette to stun the Lightning 2-1.

"Crow played great for us," Jonathan Toews said. "It's not the first time he's stolen a game for us this season."

The plot turned in Game 2. The Blackhawks carved out a 2-1 second-period lead. The Lightning responded with two markers, which included Tyler Johnson's goal-line chip shot from 3 feet out to give Tampa Bay a 3-2 lead. Jason Garrison whistled in the game-winner on the power play at the 8:49 mark, sending the series back to Chicago even at one game apiece.

"Maybe he let in a few goals that he wasn't happy with," Toews said. "At the end of the day, he's always shown that he's ready to absorb that responsibility. I don't doubt that he's going to want to bounce back."

Crawford's struggles continued in Game 3. Callahan opened the scoring with a long slapper from the top of the right circle just 5 minutes into the game. Brad Richards and Brandon Saad countered to give the Blackhawks a 2-1 edge. While Saad's goal was being announced, Crawford couldn't corral a rebound, allowing Ondrej Palat to tie the game. Cedric Paquette won it with 3:11 left. The Blackhawks now trailed in the series.

"Probably weren't my best games, the last two," Crawford said. "But then again, I can't be thinking about what happened before; gotta worry about what's next."

Crawford's moment for redemption came in Game 4. The Lightning dominated the first period, outshooting the Blackhawks 9-2. Crawford turned aside all nine shots, weathering three power plays. Toews put the Blackhawks on the board early in the second period. Twenty minutes later, Saad swatted home his own rebound for a 2-1 lead.

The Final was tied 2-2 headed back to Tampa, and Crawford would never allow the Lightning to lead in the series again.

The Châteauguay, Quebec, native sparkled in Game 5, stopping 31 of 32 shots, including all 15 in the third period against a desperate Lightning team. He was named the No. 1 star after outdueling Tampa Bay's Ben Bishop and giving the Blackhawks a chance to win the Stanley Cup on home ice for the first time in 77 years.

"Didn't start out the way I wanted, but I was able to stay with it," Crawford said afterward. "We can't get ahead of ourselves. We've got a lot of work to do here, and it's going to be an even harder battle."

Crawford's biggest save—a heartstopper for the millions watching locally and nationally—was coming.

Scoreless game. Early second period. Paquette chipped a puck over Duncan Keith to Steven Stamkos, who was alone at the red line. The talented sniper wheeled toward the net. The puck started to wobble. He corralled it. He even had time to slow down and make his move. He had Crawford going down, his momentum heading right. Stamkos darted the opposite way. The top of the cage on the far side was wide open…THUD!

At the last instant, Crawford stretched his left leg pad, denying the dangerous and desperate Stamkos.

Keith potted the Cup-clincher late in the second. Kane added some insurance. And the 30-year-old Crawford won his second Stanley Cup in three years.

A perfect ending. ▮

Kris Bryant
@KrisBryant_23

Congrats to the Hawks and the city of Chicago. Well deserved!! #StanleyCup #Champs

Frank Thomas
@TheBigHurt_35

I Just Witnessed A Dynasty Live!! #CongratsHawks

Sophia Bush
@SophiaBush

Congrats to my home-away-from-home team!! Yeah baby!

President Obama
@POTUS

Congrats to my hometown @NHLBlackhawks on 3 titles in 6 years - we'll see you and The Cup at the White House!

Chicago Bulls
@chicagobulls

Congratulations to our friends the @NHLBlackhawks on winning the #StanleyCup Championship!

Rahm Emanuel
@RahmEmanuel

Congratulations to our Stanley Cup Champion @NHLBlackhawks!! #ONEGOAL

Elena Delle Donne
@De11eDonne

#stanleycupchampions #onegoal so awesome to be at this game!!

Coach
@CMPunk

I love the @NHLBlackhawks. I love Chicago. Best team. Best city.

Chicago Fire
@NBCChicagoFire

Cheers to the champions! @NHLBlackhawks #StanleyCup

Iconic musicians, fellow athletes and other famous fans cheered on the Blackhawks during the team's historic run to the 2015 Stanley Cup. Chicago's sports teams were united by the campaign #OneCity #OneGoal, sending good luck and congratulatory messages throughout the postseason. MMA fighter CM Punk, shown wearing his "Toews Beard" tee (lower right), was one of the many celebrities who supported the team via Twitter.

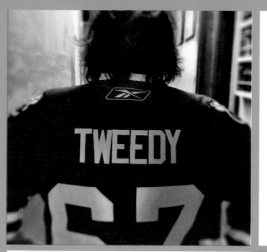

The Fratellis
@TheFratellis

You did it again didn't ya?!

JJ Watt
@JJWatt

Chicago would be a fun place to be tonight. #BecauseItsTheCup

Brian Kelly
@CoachBrianKelly

Congrats to the Blackhawks, Coach Q & GM (ND alum) Stan Bowman on the Cup win!

You & the Cup can have tix anytime!

Chicago Cubs
@Cubs

#OneCity #OneGoal

Chicago White Sox
@whitesox

#HAWKSWIN! #HAWKSWIN!

CONGRATS BLACKHAWKS

ON YOUR SIXTH STANLEY CUP

Chicago Bears
@ChicagoBears

Congrats @NHLBlackhawks on topping off another unforgettable season. - Your friends at the #Bears.

AS THE HAWKS JUST PROVED, YOU CAN BOTTLE LIGHTNING.

Chicago Fire
@ChicagoFire

Time to party Chicago!
@NHLBlackhawks
#OneCity #OneGoal #SixCups!! 🏆

Rage Against the Machine's Tom Morello and Wilco's Jeff Tweedy shared images of their personalized jerseys, while "Top Chef" winner Stephanie Izard sold Blackhawks cookies baked by Pastry Chef Mimi Rafalski in the West Loop's Little Goat. Even President Barack Obama expressed his excitement at being able to invite his hometown Blackhawks—and the Stanley Cup—back to the White House for a third time during his presidency.

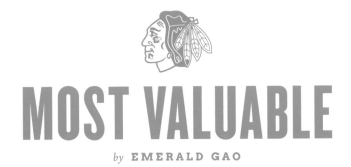

MOST VALUABLE

by EMERALD GAO

Out of everything he's accomplished in his 10-year National Hockey League career, encompassing championships and Olympic gold medals and awards, there's no question what Duncan Keith holds dearest.

"I'm proud of the three Stanley Cups—I don't think anything tops that," he said. "It's the ultimate pinnacle of success for a team, winning the Cup. The gold medals are right up there as well; it's a different mindset, a different feeling, knowing you represent your country, but I think the things you win as a team bring the most happiness."

It should come as a surprise to absolutely no one that Keith is most comfortable defining himself as a foot soldier, demurring whenever he is singled out for individual accomplishments. When NHL Commissioner Gary Bettman summoned him to the red carpet at center ice to receive the Conn Smythe Trophy late in the evening of June 15, he skated across the ice, good-naturedly ducking a few head ruffles from teammates and waving to the crowd. But when he got his hands on the hardware, the grin directed at the cameras was brief, almost perfunctory.

Was it the weight of the trophy that's handed out annually to the most valuable player of the postseason? Couldn't be, not with an even heavier, shinier beauty waiting to be hoisted just minutes later—and he did that with jubilance and triumph written all over his bearded face.

Maybe Keith was somewhat bewildered, being in the spotlight like that. After all, the Conn Smythe isn't meant to be shared, although that didn't stop him from trying.

"When you look at the names on the trophies, that's a special group and a special honor," he acknowledged. "At the same time it's very humbling. Anybody who has won those awards knows you don't get them without having great teammates and a great organization. Hockey is the ultimate team game, and you never get anything like that without being surrounded by great players."

His teammates weren't as hesitant to chime in on Keith's achievements throughout the playoffs.

"It's about time he got some recognition like that," said Brent Seabrook, Keith's longest-tenured teammate and defensive partner, and one of his best friends in hockey. "All three Cup wins, he's been a horse and a monster for us, and it's been fun to watch."

"That guy was unbelievable," said Corey Crawford, who has enjoyed one of the best views of Keith's oeuvre throughout the years. "I don't think I've seen anyone play any better."

Although Keith wasn't one of the three finalists for the Norris Trophy this past season, those in the know could make a case that he was never more important to the team than he was in 2014-15. An early injury to rookie Trevor van Riemsdyk created uncertainty in the bottom defensive pairing, which resulted in a revolving door of blueliners in the sixth spot—seven in total, including three who were traded away during the season. Rather than overburdening his top pairings, Head Coach Joel Quenneville opted for balance and predictability, rotating veteran players in with the less experienced defensemen.

According to behindthenet.ca, Keith played just 47.4 percent of his 5-on-5 minutes last season with Seabrook (compared to 86.5 percent in 2013-14). Another 22 percent was spent with veteran Michal Rozsival, meaning over 30 percent of his 5-on-5 ice time featured a varied cast of sidekicks. Keith believes the lack of consistency made him more versatile, even *more* valuable, if possible. And if the entire team seemed to get better in the playoffs, the driving force for that improvement was surely Keith, who shoulders more burden than anyone except perhaps captain Jonathan Toews.

"No one more deserving [of the Conn Smythe]," enthused Brad Richards, who's familiar with the herculean requirements of claiming that particular trophy. "Right from the first game against Nashville, I saw a different level of hockey that I'm not sure I've ever seen on my team—just how he kept doing it and never showed any signs of fatigue."

"DUNCS IS ONE OF THOSE SPECIAL ATHLETES," SEABROOK SAID. "HE'S GOT THAT SPECIAL ENGINE. HE'S A FREAK—BUT IT'S CRAZY TO SEE WHAT HE'S ABLE TO DO. HE'S PRETTY AMAZING."

Indeed, what made Keith's playoff effort so impressive was not only the depth and breadth of his contributions, but his sustained excellence throughout. He scored the double-overtime winner in the very first outing against Nashville, then added the series-winning goal late in Game 6. His 21 points tied Chris Chelios for the franchise record among defensemen in a single playoff year. Over a 23-game span, Keith drove possession regularly for the Blackhawks, posting a shot-attempt percentage south of 50 in just five outings; four of those five games were on the road, featuring largely unfavorable matchups.

He accomplished that all while becoming just the fourth player to surpass the 700-minute mark since the statistic for ice time was introduced in 1998, logging 92 more minutes than the second-most prolific skater in the postseason, Tampa Bay's Victor Hedman.

"Duncs is one of those special athletes," Seabrook said. "He's got that special engine. He's a freak—I know we've all talked about it, and the media has made a big deal about it, but it's crazy to see what he's able to do. He has his days where he's tired, his tough days, things like that, but when he gets in the zone playing hockey, I feel like he can play from puck drop to the final buzzer, stay out there for the whole game. It's fun to watch him play and see him in the dressing room and be a part of everything that he does. He's pretty amazing."

Keith's special engine was running on all cylinders leading up to the Cup-winning goal in Game 6. Surging into the zone, he took a pass from Patrick Kane just inside the blue line, snuck a snap shot through a block attempt by Cedric Paquette, then sidestepped his man to collect his own rebound and roof home the opening goal of the game—and the ultimate difference-maker.

Keith recalls another goal he once scored, in a simpler time, when the stakes were somewhat different.

"I was a kid, really young, about 11 years old, in a tournament back in Pee Wee," Keith said. "The final game had gone into overtime, and every two minutes you had to take a player off, so it ended up being two versus two in a championship game. I ended up scoring the game-winning goal. When I scored, I started to wonder what it would be like playing NHL games and scoring the game-winning goal for the Stanley Cup. That's the type of thing that's so far away that you don't really put a whole lot of thought into it.

"And I still didn't know when I scored that goal against Tampa if it was going to be the game-winning goal or not, because there was still a lot of hockey left. But it turned out that it was, and obviously I'll take it."

Keith received plenty of accolades in the immediate aftermath of Game 6—"Best defenseman in the world," insisted Patrick Sharp, Keith's other best friend in hockey. But such an achievement can be difficult to process, let alone describe in words. Months later, Keith merely offers that he is "proud" of being a three-time champion before changing the subject to speak of the future.

"I still have a lot of hockey left," the 32-year-old said. "We've got a great organization, and I think there's still a lot of opportunities to win more. It's not a feeling that everything's done and finished now; it's a feeling that we're proud of winning and having those three Cups, but also knowing that there's still work to be done."

Keith says that he was able to follow up on his shot in Game 6 because of his momentum on the initial drive. Momentum seems to take Keith a lot of places, from Fort Frances to Chicago, with stops in British Columbia, Michigan and Norfolk. The work ethic he developed in 2005, at the start of his rookie year, is the same work ethic he brings to the rink 10 years later.

"The only thing that's changed from 10 years ago is knowing the potential that we have," Keith said. "My first few years in the league, I was just trying to establish myself and trying to fit in. Now I'm going into the season with the mindset of winning a Stanley Cup."

Keith and Seabrook are the only players, along with the now-departed Sharp, who can describe how unrecognizably different the Blackhawks were 10 years ago.

"My first year in the league with Duncan—it wasn't a very good hockey club," Seabrook said. "Obviously things have changed; once we got the ball rolling, it was cool to see how loud that building would get and how good we could play. It was one of those things, like catching fire. Being able to win Stanley Cups is a lifelong dream, but starting out 10 years ago, I don't think either of us could have told you it would have been like this."

"Our first few years in the league we played Detroit a lot," Keith added. "I admired guys like Kris Draper and Kirk Maltby just as much as I did Steve Yzerman and Niklas

Lidstrom, just because those guys had played together for so long and been a part of so many winning teams. They were just winners. Me and Brent and Patrick—and I think those two would say the same thing—learned so much from those teams and those players. It's cool to think that we've been part of a team like that for 10 years now, and cool to know that feeling of playing with some guys for so long and having success with one organization."

A decade is a long time, but Keith appreciates how fleeting a career in professional hockey can be.

"Every year just flies by, goes by faster and faster," he said. "I don't know why that is, but the years just keep piling on, and that reinforces the fact that you only have one career and you want to make the most of it, win while you have that chance. That was a big part of why we put that pressure on ourselves this year."

Pressure from both within and without turned Keith's most outstanding season into a personal crucible. In addition to a difficult separation from his wife and son, he and the rest of the team suffered an unknowable loss just before Christmas when Clint Reif, beloved assistant equipment manager whom Keith was particularly close to, died. Two months later, former teammate Steve Montador also passed away.

Reif left behind a wife, four children and a shell-shocked locker room, and Montador still had close friends in the organization. While there was a league-wide mourning period for both individuals, the Blackhawks agreed that any victory that should occur in mid-June would be dedicated to Reif.

For Keith, that win—that historic, cathartic moment in a United Center whose interior was battered by noise a few hours after its exterior was battered by rain—was missing only one thing.

"In a perfect world, it would have been nice just to have Clint out on the ice celebrating with us," he said. "That's more of the feeling that I had, anyway, just thinking how nice it would have been to be able to have a beer with him and how happy he would be about winning at home. He should have been right there with us, celebrating on the ice instead of up high in the sky."

As a symbol, the Stanley Cup never loses its power, no matter how many times it's been touched. Winning it is a reasonable thing to imagine as a child, when extraordinary feats seem hazily attainable, but in reality, becoming a Stanley Cup champion requires a level of sacrifice, determination and fortitude that's nearly unmatched in professional sports. Still, when the trophy is secured, the euphoria is powerful enough to reduce grownups to children once more.

Keith, like many hockey players, will not discuss his own legacy before the time is right, but consciously or not, his most recent Cup celebration served as homage to his own roots as well as the roots he's started to lay down as a player and as a father.

Instead of Penticton, B.C., where he calls home in the offseason, Keith took the Stanley Cup to Fort Frances, Ontario, this past summer. The Keiths moved there from Winnipeg when Duncan was just 1, and virtually his entire childhood was spent at the outdoor rink.

"It's basically where I learned to play hockey," Keith explained. "So it was a no-brainer; I didn't take it back there the first couple times, and I felt kind of guilty about that, so I was really excited to be able to win a third time and do that."

During Keith's visit, he noted the addition of a second rink, impressive for a town with a population of less than 8,000. It's a sign of how much hockey has grown in the area, undoubtedly influenced by its most successful export. In that way, Keith's third Cup is also about instilling that same simple dream in the next generation.

For Keith, it starts with his son, Colton, who was a swaddled newborn when the Blackhawks won in 2013 but has graduated to skates and slap shots around the living room in the two years since.

"He knows what the Stanley Cup is, he knows what the Blackhawks are, he loves coming to the games and watching, he loves coming down to the glass for warmups," Keith said. "We've watched videos of some of the games, and he knows, he's a smart little guy."

The resemblance between Colton and his father is never more evident than in a photo taken of them after Game 6, two sets of teeth bared joyfully for the camera as they teamed up to hoist the Cup. Duncan bore most of the weight, as he's accustomed to doing, but Colton was able to get both outstretched hands on the trophy.

After all, the Stanley Cup doesn't have a notice that proclaims "You Must Be This Tall to Dream." ▥

ABOVE AND OPPOSITE: Blackhawks babies celebrate in and around the Stanley Cup, including (clockwise) Ames Desjardins, Léonna Vermette, Theo Hjalmarsson, Austin Carcillo, Makayla Bickell and Jaxson Versteeg.

WE ARE THE CHAMPIONS

by BOB VERDI

Hairy and hugging, the Blackhawks broke into song on the morning of Tuesday, June 16. They stood by their stalls, a chorus line of arms around shoulders, to serenade themselves and assembled guests.

"WE ARE THE CHAMPIONS!" they screeched, wearing as proof T-shirts and hats hot off the presses. "WE ARE THE CHAMPIONS!"

Not long ago, this franchise was invisible. Now Chicago's boys of winter are indivisible and, as is their wont, ahead of the curve. Their United Center locker room was scheduled to undergo a complete makeover this summer. So after winning a third Stanley Cup in six years on Monday night, the guys fast-forwarded the reconstruction. A few ceiling tiles were popped loose, the carpet took on serious moisture, and cigar smoke furnished an aroma of success.

Families and friends surrounded tubs of bubbly and beer for hours after a milestone 2-0 victory over the Tampa Bay Lightning. It was a standing-room-only crowd of 22,424, even for those who had secured precious seats but rarely used them. Fans were wetly whooshed into the building under a tornado warning, then were reluctant to depart after a nine-month odyssey concluded just as they hoped it would.

The Blackhawks are as dependable as your best friend, your dog, your couch. After 105 games, 23 in the playoffs, they clinched before their beloved fans for the first time since 1938. At that time the Stanley Cup was resting in Toronto because there was no way that team would upset the mighty Maple Leafs, especially after locating an emergency goalie and extricating him from a saloon to play the series opener.

But that Monday night, the silver trophy was there for the organization that is hockey's gold standard. The mere visage of a table being brought to center ice after the handshake line elicited an ovation. Duncan Keith, who scored the winner on his own rebound, received the

Conn Smythe Trophy by unanimous vote. A remarkable +16 in the playoffs, Keith is perpetual motion. But finally he came to a halt after skating so many miles and stood in place. Teammates say there's nothing they haven't seen the tireless defenseman do, except yawn.

Guardians in white gloves carried forth the 35-pound Stanley Cup. Captain Jonathan Toews hoisted it, as he did in Philadelphia in 2010 and in Boston in 2013. Then Toews did what great leaders do: He handed the prize to Kimmo Timonen, 40, an elegant defenseman who can now retire with a smile on his face.

"When he told me this morning that if we win I would get it next, I almost cried," said Timonen, who was diagnosed with blood clots last summer, but took a chance with the Blackhawks as they took a chance with him at the trading deadline.

"I almost didn't know what to do with the Cup when I got it. It was my first time. It's been a long journey. I didn't even know if I could ever play again after that health scare, but I wanted to give it one more shot. Now I'm living a dream. I'm a Stanley Cup champion. I can't ask for anything more than that.

"There are so many words I want to say. But I'm leaving this game happy, relieved, ready. I didn't do much here. I just made sure the water bottles were full. I just wanted to be a part of this team, and I have never seen a team like this one."

Timonen handed off the Cup to Antoine Vermette, an expensive trade-deadline acquisition whose contributions were priceless. Brad Richards was next. He'd assisted on both scores that night, including Patrick Kane's late in the third period. That tally created the only two-goal separation of the entire Final against a maimed but spirited Lightning crew.

"A year ago I'm down on myself, feeling like I'm the lowest human being on the planet," mused Richards, who shut off his phone after the Blackhawks called with a free-agent contract offer last summer. "Now I'm passing the puck to Patrick Kane [and winning the Cup] with a truly special group of people. If it weren't for the salary cap, half the guys in the National Hockey League would want to be in Chicago."

Everybody was drenched in the locker room, where communal spraying verified the Blackhawks' code: sink or swim together. Rocky Wirtz, the chairman who was accorded a roar of approval when he lifted the Cup on the ice, told the young men of the pride he felt in their work ethic. They thanked the boss by putting him through a veritable car wash from green bottles. John McDonough, the president and CEO, extolled the players for making history. They reminded him that the season was over, and gave him the business too.

"Some of these games were so brutally close," said McDonough, wearing what once was a very nice suit. "I mean, three goals by Anaheim [in the Western Conference Final] in 37 seconds! Torture. But these guys are wonderful. They've done so much, yet there is no big-league swagger, no arrogance. They are so likable. They are the most approachable players in professional sports. And this team exemplifies the selflessness that makes our game so unique."

Head Coach Joel Quenneville stepped forward to utter a few words—very few—before he was emphatically hooted off stage.

"I told you they don't listen to my speeches," groused Q with towel in hand. Nearby stood assistant Mike Kitchen, who joined the staff the summer after the 2010 Cup. He knew none of the players. Now Kitchen raves about how the core group has matured. What's unsaid, however, is the atmosphere encouraged by Quenneville. He lets the locker room breathe, so personalities can evolve, so leaders can grow. Quenneville repeatedly recognizes "No. 19, a special guy." But Jonathan Toews defers.

"I get way too much credit as captain," he said. "When you fall behind 3-0 in a game and maybe you're getting outshot 10-3, and you look down the bench and you see guys who are poised, calm, confident, that's a pretty good feeling. I'm not going to lie: Game 6 was the most pressure I think I've ever felt going into a game. You're trying to erase thoughts of having to go back to Tampa for a seventh game, the momentum they would have.

"But we have a way of taking things in stride. When we fell behind 3-2 in the Anaheim series, we didn't think of having to win two games. We thought about winning the next shift, the next period, the next game. We don't think about the aftermath. We know what works. Take it one piece at a time, even when things are going south. We are a hard team to play against, to beat four times in two weeks. We don't pay attention to a lot of the stuff that you hear. How our top four defensemen couldn't possibly handle all the minutes they were playing without wearing out. How no human beings could withstand the physical pounding our guys were taking game after game in a long series. We don't worry about that. And we don't panic. Nobody on this team freaks out.

"I used to overreact. I used to get really emotional. During the playoffs in 2013, I lost it in Detroit in Game 4. We were down in the series, and I took three straight penalties. But Seabs came over to me in the box and calmed me down. 'Everything is going to be OK. But we need you.' That's what I mean about leaders. It's not just me. No way. Brent's one. They're all over this room."

After getting the hook, Quenneville ducked into his office, where his mother, Gloria, beamed as her son pointed to a board where names are attached by metallic strips according to lines or defensive pairings. One by one, he pointed out individuals, mentioning their roles, occasionally applying the word "freak" to compliment the

"THEY PUSHED ME TO THE FRONT OF THE GROUP," DESJARDINS SAID. "BLEW ME AWAY. NO CHANCE. I'M THE FIFTH GUY TO CARRY THE STANLEY CUP? ON THIS TEAM....COULDN'T BELIEVE IT. BUT THAT TELLS YOU WHAT THIS BUNCH OF GUYS IS ALL ABOUT."

OPPOSITE: Twelve-year veteran Antoine Vermette enjoys his first moments as a Stanley Cup champion.
ABOVE TOP: Patrick Sharp passes the Cup to fellow three-time champion Niklas Hjalmarsson.
ABOVE BOTTOM: Rookie Trevor van Riemsdyk kisses the Cup after returning from injury to play the last four games of the Final.

likes of Toews and Keith. Then Quenneville stopped at Andrew Shaw.

"His back seized up this morning," Q mentioned. "Couldn't move. Didn't know whether he could go tonight. Spent the whole day here with our unbelievable medical staff and trainers. Did he go tonight? Did he do what all these guys do? Sacrifice for each other? We fall behind in a lot of series, down 2-1 or whatever. But they adjust, get better as it goes along and find a way. They find a frigging way. Amazing."

Earlier, as Richards completed his moment with the Cup, Andrew Desjardins felt a nudge from teammates. At the trade deadline, he was another big catch whose arrival in Chicago was announced in small print.

"They pushed me to the front of the group," Desjardins said. "Blew me away. No chance. I'm the fifth guy to carry the Stanley Cup? On this team. Jonny to Kimmo to Vermy to Richie to me? Couldn't believe it. But that tells you what this bunch of guys is all about. I'm sure it was the big guys who made it happen like that, and I completely tip my hat to them. Fifth!

"When I came here, I knew how to play hockey. I think I had a winning attitude, but I feel like here is where I learned how to win. I didn't know what to expect, coming from San Jose with a baby son. All these great players, so many unknowns. But I started getting some minutes in pressure situations, which is what I like. My confidence went way up here because I felt they trusted me. I became somewhat important.

"You only hold the Stanley Cup for a few seconds, but it means so much. That thing could be addictive. It's crazy how this ended up for me. But this is a different group. A few weeks after I got here, I went home to my wife, Mandy, and I told her: These guys not only play better, they eat better, they take care of what they put into their bodies. You don't win a Stanley Cup at the dinner table, and I still have a couple beers at night. But in the morning, instead of bacon and eggs, maybe I'll have a health drink."

In the postgame ceremony, National Hockey League Commissioner Gary Bettman anointed the Blackhawks a dynasty. Wirtz amended that slightly to a "reinvention," given how the rosters of his three championship teams have undergone change, sometimes radical, out of necessity. Scotty Bowman, the Blackhawks' Hall of Fame senior

advisor who was fitted for his 14th ring, seized both sides of the semantic debate. He coached the 2002 Detroit Red Wings to their third Cup in six years, but they had an outsized payroll.

"Now with the salary cap, it's all different," Bowman said. "The 10 days we had off before the Anaheim series, important. But to do that, we had to sweep Minnesota. Top four defensemen, terrific. And how about the goalie?"

Corey Crawford stood there, his record speaking for itself. He was pulled after one period of the playoff opener in Nashville, took a shot that dented his mask and dazed him against Minnesota, then got buffeted by low-hanging Ducks before chloroforming the Lightning in the Final. Tampa Bay, the league's most offensive aggregation, managed 10 goals in six playoff games and just two in the last three. Steven Stamkos had an excellent crack at his first goal of the Final in Game 6, but when he came upon a meandering puck, slowed, faked and went deep, Crawford smothered the effort with his outstretched pad.

"You look at all the articles before the series in the postseason," noted Jimmy Waite, the goalie coach. "And when they get to Corey and whomever he's up against, the other guy gets the check. He gives his team the edge in goal. The other team is supposed to have the advantage. But then

OPPOSITE TOP: Marian Hossa snaps a selfie with Brad Richards.
OPPOSITE BOTTOM: Jonathan Toews, Patrick Sharp, Daniel Carcillo, Joakim Nordstrom and Marcus Kruger hug it out.
ABOVE: VP/GM Stan Bowman and father Scotty celebrate their third Stanley Cup as members of the Blackhawks front office.

"THIS ISN'T NORMAL," JOHNNY ODUYA SUGGESTED. "WE FEEL IT'S MEANT TO BE, BECAUSE THAT'S JUST THE WAY IT IS AROUND HERE. THREE IN SIX YEARS. THIS ISN'T NORMAL."

when the series is over, who's the winning goalie? Corey doesn't pay attention to that. He just plays for the guys and they play for him.

"He's got a quality that great goalies have to have. He lets in a bad goal, like all goalies do, and he just gets over it. Forgets it. Plus, in the Anaheim series, he was so composed. The Ducks go to the net a lot. I feel they could have had a few obstruction penalties, but even when Corey was interfered with, he never lost it. You show the other team that you're frustrated, that they're in your head, they've won."

After core veterans arranged the Cup lift for those aforementioned newcomers—Timonen, Vermette, Richards and Desjardins—Kane got the honors. He returned from a serious collarbone injury in late February just in time to join the playoff push, and reunited with Stanley in his corner of the room for several minutes. They've become quite friendly.

"I think everyone was so happy, celebrating with our closest friends and family in our own locker room, they kind of forgot about the Cup for a moment," said Kane, who attracted attention from two Lightning skaters before sliding a fine pass to Keith for the first and winning goal.

"I don't think there was any way we were losing with our group, at home, with the crowd buzzing," he added. "After that first goal by Duncs, the energy in the building was outrageous. The second goal, I could watch that clip a million times and it will never get old."

The Blackhawks played four different series against four different styles. They played 23 games, plus 151 minutes and 23 seconds of sudden death. No wonder Marcus Kruger appeared famished and thin. When the

season starts, he leaves his ego back in Stockholm and rarely logs a bad shift let alone a bad game. He scored the winner in the longest game in franchise history: Game 2 in Anaheim, at 16:12 of the sixth period.

Demure Niklas Hjalmarsson, one of the four "Minute Men" on the blue line, shed his gear, relieved. Hjalmarsson blocked 23 shots in the Final, not counting the occasions when he clogged lanes, usually against the most dangerous adversaries. He is the Blackhawks' shutdown specialist, and now that he could shut it down for a few months, Hjalmarsson quietly inquired about the location of the cigar concession. Beside him was Johnny Oduya, who incurred a tear in his left elbow in Game 3 of the Final, not that you would know it. He was terrific.

"This isn't normal," Oduya suggested. "We feel it's meant to be, because that's just the way it is around here. Three in six years. This isn't normal."

He and his fellow countrymen gathered for a picture. Then a couple of them, David Rundblad and Joakim Nordstrom, peeled off and headed toward the hot tub, the largest of many puddles in the room. Kris Versteeg, the team disc jockey who selects music that blasts throughout the United Center during warmups, was in the middle of everything. Marian Hossa, the ultimate professional, took it all in like a grade school teacher watching kids frolic during recess.

"This is really a great group of guys," he said. "This group really cares about each other."

Then there was Teuvo Teravainen, half the age of fellow Finn Timonen, staring at his Chicago father figure.

"He helped me a lot," said the prodigy, rubbing his bare chin. "Now I can shave this beard off." ▥

OPPOSITE: How Swede it is! Countrymen Marcus Kruger, Johnny Oduya, Joakim Nordstrom, Viktor Svedberg, David Rundblad and Niklas Hjalmarsson pose together with the Cup.

OPPOSITE TOP: Blackhawks fans party outside Wrigley Field following the Game 6 victory.
OPPOSITE BOTTOM: Dynamic duo Jonathan Toews and Patrick Kane lift the Cup together on the ice.
ABOVE TOP LEFT: Assistant Athletic Trainer Jeff Thomas raises the Cup.
ABOVE TOP RIGHT: Equipment Manager Troy Parchman enjoys some family time with wife, Whitney, and son, Evan.
ABOVE BOTTOM: Massage Therapist Pawel Prylinski, a 22-year Blackhawks veteran, smiles with his daughter, son and the Cup.

ABOVE TOP: After celebrating on the ice, Jonathan Toews moves the Cup—and the party—inside the locker room.
ABOVE BOTTOM: No scars to soak up the champagne this time! Andrew Shaw pops a bottle of bubbly.
OPPOSITE TOP: Assistant Equipment Manager Jim Heintzelman gets sprayed while hoisting the Cup.
OPPOSITE BOTTOM: Viktor Svedberg soaks teammates, including (right to left) Marian Hossa, Patrick Sharp and Duncan Keith.

OPPOSITE TOP: Marian Hossa and Patrick Sharp sustain some more spray.
OPPOSITE BOTTOM: Kyle Cumiskey and David Rundblad cheer on Kris Versteeg.
ABOVE TOP: Rundblad pours a drink for Assistant Coach Kevin Dineen.
ABOVE BOTTOM: Senior Director of Team Services Tony Ommen gets in on the fun.

OPPOSITE TOP: Head Athletic Trainer Mike Gapski is the center of attention thanks to his silver friend.
OPPOSITE BOTTOM: Strength and Conditioning Coach Paul Goodman enjoys a quiet moment with Brandon Saad, Johnny Oduya, Niklas Hjalmarsson and Viktor Svedberg.
ABOVE TOP: President and CEO John McDonough pours some beer while Coach Q tries to keep his cigar dry.
ABOVE BOTTOM: Vice President of Hockey Operations Al MacIsaac poses with GM of Minor League Affiliations Mark Bernard, Senior Director of Amateur Scouting Mark Kelley and Vice President/General Manager Stan Bowman.

ABOVE TOP: Patrick Sharp helps Brandon Saad get even more soaked.
ABOVE BOTTOM: Chairman Rocky Wirtz shares a word with Corey Crawford.
OPPOSITE TOP: Scott Darling snaps a fired-up selfie with Joakim Nordstrom and the Cup.
OPPOSITE BOTTOM: Brent Seabrook, Jonathan Toews, Marian Hossa, Duncan Keith, Sharp and Patrick Kane—six of the seven Blackhawks who have won three championships since 2010—pose with the Cup.

ABOVE TOP: Coach Q celebrates with his staff: Video Coach Matt Meacham, Goaltending Coach Jimmy Waite, Assistant Coach Kevin Dineen and Assistant Coach Mike Kitchen.
ABOVE BOTTOM: The last two Blackhawks Conn Smythe winners, Duncan Keith and Patrick Kane, enjoy a moment with the Cup.

CHAMPIONSHIP BELT WINNERS

ROUND 1 • GAME 1
SCOTT DARLING

ROUND 1 • GAME 3
MARIAN HOSSA

ROUND 1 • GAME 4
BRENT SEABROOK

ROUND 1 • GAME 6
COREY CRAWFORD

ROUND 2 • GAME 1
TEUVO TERAVAINEN

ROUND 2 • GAME 2
PATRICK KANE

ROUND 2 • GAME 3
MARIAN HOSSA

ROUND 2 • GAME 4
COREY CRAWFORD

ROUND 3 • GAME 2
MARCUS KRUGER

ROUND 3 • GAME 4
ANTOINE VERMETTE

ROUND 3 • GAME 6
ANDREW SHAW

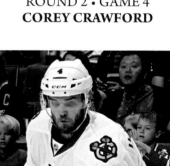

ROUND 3 • GAME 7
NIKLAS HJALMARSSON

ROUND 4 • GAME 1
ANTOINE VERMETTE

ROUND 4 • GAME 4
BRANDON SAAD

ROUND 4 • GAME 5
KRIS VERSTEEG

ROUND 4 • GAME 6
C.J. REIF

2015 STANLEY CUP PLAYOFFS

PLAYER	POS	GP	G	A	PTS	+/-	PIM	PP	SH	GW	S	TOI
PATRICK KANE	RW	23	11	12	23	7	0	2	0	3	64	20:23
DUNCAN KEITH	D	23	3	18	21	16	4	0	0	3	59	31:06
JONATHAN TOEWS	C	23	10	11	21	7	8	3	1	0	61	20:54
MARIAN HOSSA	RW	23	4	13	17	7	10	1	1	2	69	19:51
PATRICK SHARP	LW	23	5	10	15	2	8	1	0	0	64	15:34
BRAD RICHARDS	C	23	3	11	14	4	8	1	0	0	50	16:43
ANDREW SHAW	RW	23	5	7	12	-4	36	2	0	0	45	15:33
BRENT SEABROOK	D	23	7	4	11	5	10	1	0	1	44	26:17
BRANDON SAAD	LW	23	8	3	11	5	6	0	1	2	59	20:16
TEUVO TERAVAINEN	C	18	4	6	10	2	0	1	0	1	26	13:28
ANTOINE VERMETTE	C	20	4	3	7	5	4	0	0	3	16	13:07
NIKLAS HJALMARSSON	D	23	1	5	6	6	8	0	0	0	24	26:02
JOHNNY ODUYA	D	23	0	5	5	-4	6	0	0	0	28	24:45
BRYAN BICKELL	LW	18	0	5	5	3	14	0	0	0	18	14:33
ANDREW DESJARDINS	LW	21	1	3	4	-4	4	0	0	0	28	13:55
MARCUS KRUGER	C	23	2	2	4	-5	4	0	0	1	27	15:05
KRIS VERSTEEG	LW	12	1	1	2	2	6	0	0	0	23	13:21
MICHAL ROZSIVAL	D	10	0	1	1	-2	6	0	0	0	5	17:26
KIMMO TIMONEN	D	18	0	0	0	1	10	0	0	0	6	8:39
KYLE CUMISKEY	D	9	0	0	0	-3	0	0	0	0	1	9:28
DAVID RUNDBLAD	D	5	0	0	0	2	0	0	0	0	2	7:29
JOAKIM NORDSTROM	LW	3	0	0	0	-3	0	0	0	0	3	13:14
TREVOR VAN RIEMSDYK	D	4	0	0	0	-1	0	0	0	0	1	7:02

GOALTENDER	GP	MIN	GAA	W-L	OT	SO	SA	GA	SV%	G	A	PIM
COREY CRAWFORD	20	1,223	2.31	13-6	1	2	616	47	.924	0	0	0
SCOTT DARLING	5	298	2.21	3-1	0	0	171	11	.936	0	0	0

CELEBRATING STANLEY

CHAPTER FIVE

THEY ONLY GET BETTER

by BOB VERDI

You know the Blackhawks are on a roll when, by jogging your short-term memory, you can actually compare and rank their championship parades.

Grant Park was swell in 2013, but when did they paint all the seats at Soldier Field red? In 2010, were there this many helicopters following the caravan? If it was sunnier at the other two, didn't the most recent celebration seem busier, louder? And all those leashed dogs in the happy horde. Think of it: Many of them weren't born when this reign began. No wonder their tails were wagging.

These galas don't get old, they only get better. Once, critics insisted there were maybe 18,000 or so hockey enthusiasts in Chicago. Now even the most curmudgeonly souls must upgrade that to maybe 3 or 4 million.

From mid-morning takeoff at the United Center, through the streets of a region galvanized by this championship team, a procession of buses and trolleys drew roars of appreciation from layers of humanity that grew thicker every block. If you weren't wearing Blackhawks regalia, you needed a note from your doctor.

Judging by the hundreds of hard hats in the gallery, construction screeched to halt. Chicago's finest—the police, the backbone of this city—made it happen while nobody else appeared to be working. Desks emptied in office buildings, pictures were snapped from behind sealed windows, and when final crowd estimates are in, do all those pets count?

The last double-decker in the expedition, No. 26, contained Patrick Kane and Corey Crawford. Kane exhorted the throngs, as if they needed prompting, while the trail vehicle blew through red lights. Goalies habitually flinch at those, but Crawford hadn't seen many lately. He was extremely stingy throughout a Stanley Cup Final that was settled with his 2-0 masterpiece in Game 6 against the Tampa Bay Lightning three nights earlier.

"COR-EY! COR-EY! COR-EY!" went the chant, and these were not fair-weather fans, not after a morning cloudburst confirmed a very iffy forecast. The Blackhawks can't walk on water, but if you freeze it, they are masters of their craft. This is a matter of record, that the franchise has become a paradigm in professional sports. But look past those restraining fences and down side alleys. Has any team increased its audience so exponentially over such a relatively short period of time?

"I just can't get over it—the passion here is amazing," said Brad Richards, who has been around awhile. As he spoke, in the bowels of Soldier Field, the place was packed. The motorcade had landed, a video presentation of the Blackhawks' two-month playoff run followed, Jim Cornelison performed his patented "Star-Spangled Banner" and fireworks ensued.

Hall of Fame broadcaster Pat Foley took the microphone as only he can, and introductions began. Rocky Wirtz, the chairman, received an ovation that owners elsewhere might hear in their dreams. He declared that this Stanley Cup, won at home, felt special. Even Rocky was floored by the complete vivification of his family's franchise. Forever respectful of his father, Bill, Rocky suggested, "Dad would have been proud of the results, if not some of our methods."

John McDonough, the president and CEO, glanced at the 35-pound silver beauty shining brightly at center stage in the north end zone where the Bears play football.

Appropriately, McDonough paid homage to supporters in an open-air environment, because as the saying goes, "Sunlight is the best disinfectant." During his tenure, the Blackhawks have not only raised the bar, but eliminated the ceiling. Reflective of their stature, they are annually in demand outdoors, too. With McDonough pushing hard, the Blackhawks hosted the 2009 Winter Classic at Wrigley Field, a function widely perceived as their coming-out party after years of hibernation.

In 2014, at this very Soldier Field, the Blackhawks staged a snowy Stadium Series rout of the Pittsburgh Penguins. Last New Year's Day, the Blackhawks visited

"WE SHARE THIS WITH YOU, THE BEST FANS IN THE WORLD," CAPTAIN JONATHAN TOEWS EXCLAIMED. "MAYBE THE ONLY WAY IT DOES GET BETTER IS IF WE WIN FOUR! LET'S GO!"

the Washington Capitals in another Winter Classic. In 2016, the Blackhawks will travel to TCF Bank Stadium in Minneapolis for a league-leading fourth alfresco game, a Stadium Series encounter against the Minnesota Wild.

"If my math is correct, this is 'One Goal,' three times," McDonough told the red sea of 65,000. "This is your Stanley Cup."

Scotty Bowman? Back in the day, members of the dynastic New York Yankees calculated yearly salaries by including the World Series winners' share. Bowman has won so many Stanley Cups, he arranges them by zip code. Three of his 14 rings were secured in Chicago—with the Montreal Canadiens in 1973, Pittsburgh Penguins in 1992 and now, as senior advisor to hockey operations, with the Blackhawks, for whom his son has claimed three as vice president/general manager.

"No matter what happens, I can't catch up," Stan noted. "I'm still 11 behind."

Duncan Keith's inexhaustible form on skates is the obverse of his mode off ice, where he exhibits a low pilot light. As if reading items off a grocery list, he cordially conducts postgame interviews in a monotone, one decibel above a whisper. Perhaps that is how he conserves his energy. But when Keith was summoned to the podium, his brief remarks were delayed by a booming roar stretching from the upper deck to ground-level seats.

"MVP! MVP! MVP!"

The world-class defenseman, so often so mobile, took his Conn Smythe Trophy for a brief stroll, then talked about arriving here a decade ago and not daring to fantasize about such a love-in. A lot of main arteries were blocked off that day, but all the boys of winter agreed

that energy is a two-way street around here. They feed off those who feed off them.

"Let's keep this red machine going, baby," Keith rasped. "Let's do it again. Four sounds better than three." Later he downplayed individual accomplishments by saying, "You don't get these awards without being on great teams with great players, and I'm just proud to be part of this group of guys who care so much and do whatever it takes."

We hardly knew ye, Kimmo Timonen, but what approbation he received. At 40, he finally scaled the top of the mountain. Antoine Vermette, another trade-deadline acquisition, was a big help. At the celebration, he had wide eyes.

"These guys, they only care about winning," said Vermette, who became a father for the second time only days after he became a Stanley Cup champion for the first time. "I've never seen anything like it."

The coach, Joel Quenneville, could run for mayor, and Rahm Emanuel was there, too. The peerless captain, Jonathan Toews, didn't bring all of his voice to the ceremony. But, as usual, he said everything right and struck all the high notes.

"We share this with you, the best fans in the world," Toews exclaimed. "Maybe the only way it does get better is if we win four! Let's go!"

The captain expanded on his refusal to acknowledge the law of averages in an ultra-competitive NHL governed by an airtight salary cap.

"A lot of people are doubting us because we're going to lose key players," Toews said. "But it's happened before, and we keep finding ways to rebound. We all know we're part of the best organization in sports, and we play for the

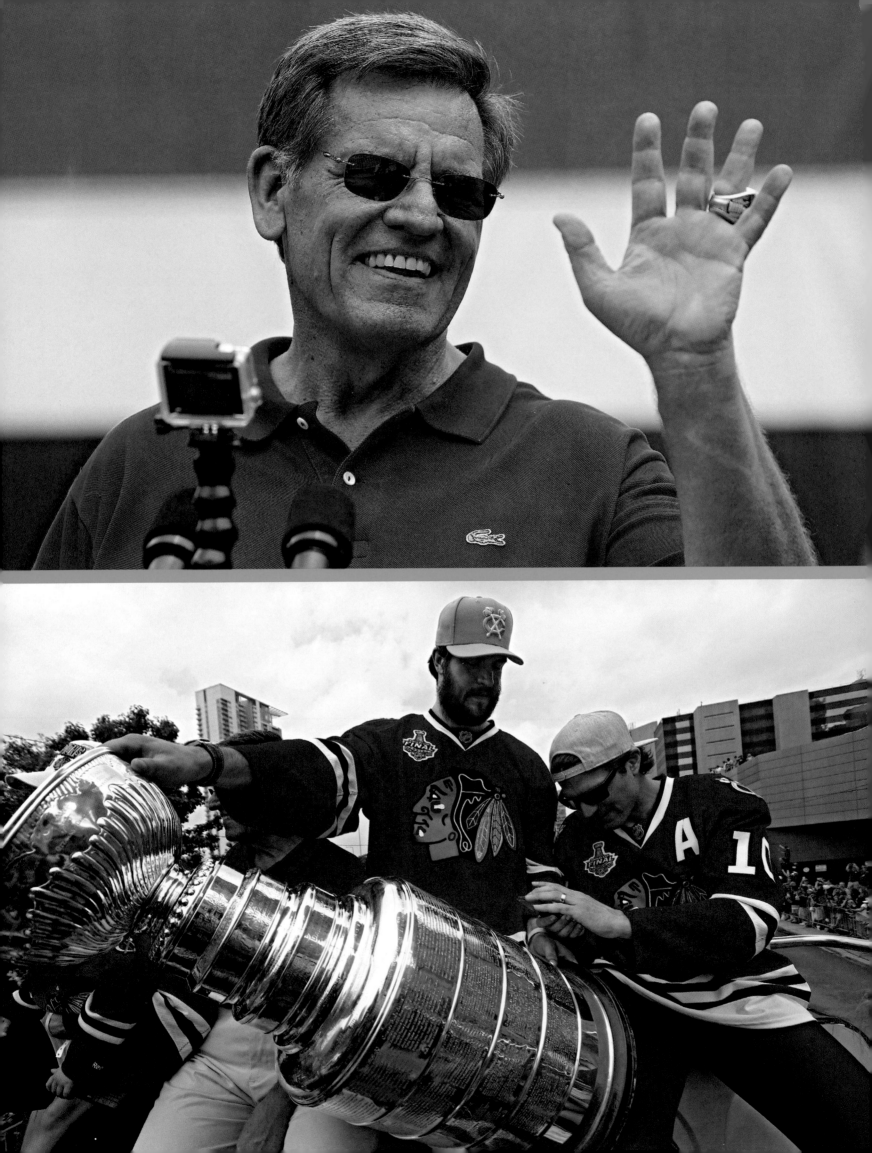

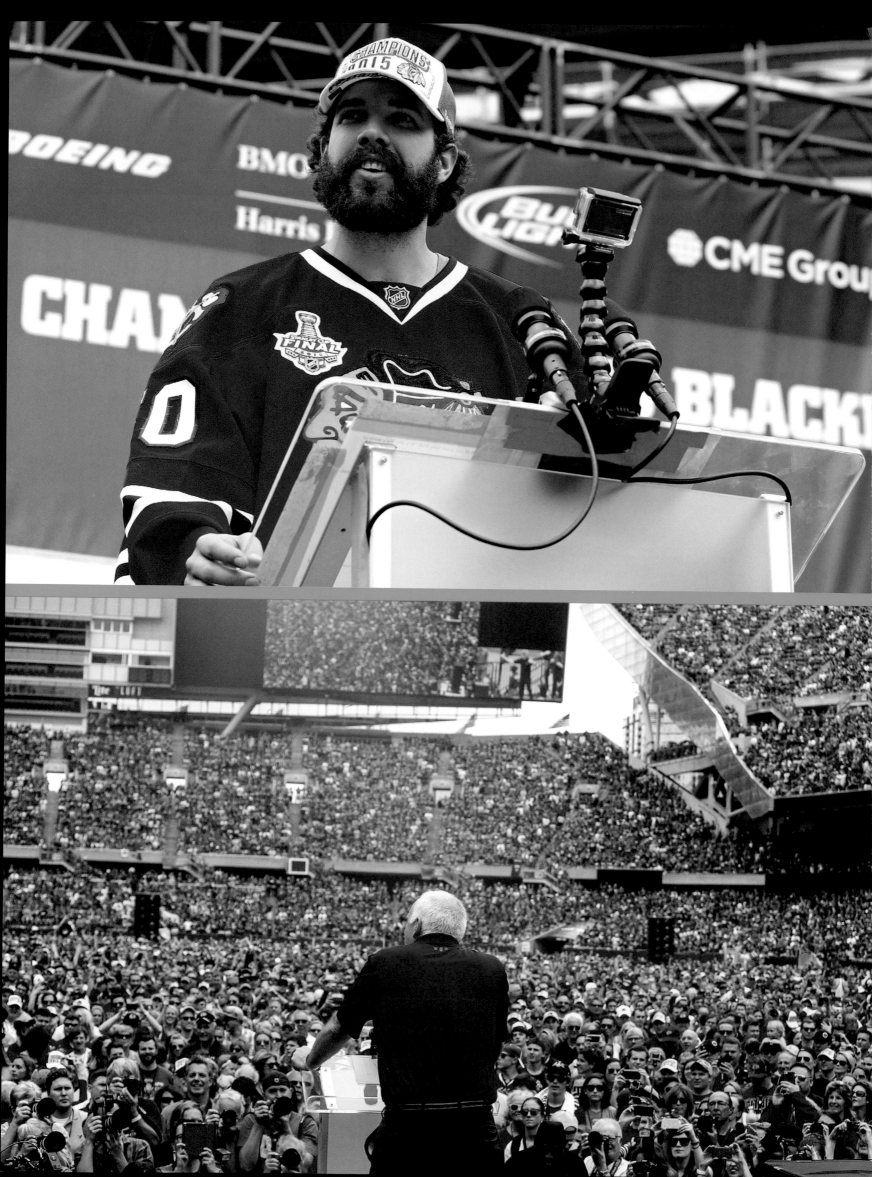

best fans in all of sports."

One of the faces in the crowd was Bryan Toews, Jonathan's father, who exuded pride.

"He always had his goals," the elder Toews said. "When Jonathan was 12 or so, he told me, 'I'm not only going to make it to the NHL, I'm going to be a star so I can buy you a new truck.'"

Then there was Kris Versteeg, who earned the championship belt after a triumphant Game 5 in Tampa Bay. The guys were otherwise occupied for several hours upon the Cup-clinching postgame party, so he was not commissioned to hand off the memento to a successor. But now the time had come, and Versteeg introduced the next holder of the belt.

C.J. Reif, the 9-year-old son of Clint, the Blackhawks' assistant equipment manager who passed away in December, came forward. The players adored Clint. On the day after Christmas, a day off, they trekked en masse to a funeral home to say goodbye. The Blackhawks dealt with serial challenges this season. But they'll see the Nashville Predators and Anaheim Ducks and St. Louis Blues again. Sadly, Clint Reif forever will be an absent friend. Versteeg wrapped C.J. in his arms and lifted him off his feet.

"This one's for Reifer," volunteered Keith, who was crushed when his pal perished.

Trevor van Riemsdyk, the rookie defenseman, will not require a facelift in his dotage. He is gifted with a permanent smile. But to be honored on this day as a Stanley Cup champion, after joining the Blackhawks as an undrafted free agent, even an educated young man such as he groped for proper nouns and adjectives.

"What would the odds have been?" TVR said. "A year and a half ago, I broke my ankle in college. Then I show up for training camp, make the team, and now I'm here with the Stanley Cup. You grow up in the driveway in New Jersey, you're 5 or 6, and you dream of winning the Stanley Cup. Thank goodness my family and friends took pictures when I got to hold it on the ice at the United Center. I pretty much blacked out. I don't really remember it, yet I'll never forget it.

"It's the coolest trophy in sports, and it means so much to Americans, Canadians, Europeans—anybody who plays hockey—because hockey is the ultimate team sport.

There's a special bond in hockey because of how hard it is, because of the culture of sacrifice. Blocking shots, taking hits, making hits, playing hurt. All for the good of the group. This is a dream. It's not supposed to happen this way, to play after getting injured early in the season, then again in April. Bad karma. But sulking gets you nowhere. And to still be able to have a small, small, small role in this, I am so lucky. Surreal."

With newcomers such as TVR and Scott Darling injected into the veteran mix, the Blackhawks present a daunting obstacle for National Hockey League rivals. Toews is 27, not 37. Keith is 31, but plays like he's 21 and could play until he's 41. Crawford is in his prime. You could go on and on, but the reality is that the core will remain intact for the near future, as will the ethos to win throughout the organization. Ponder this statistic: Toews and Kane each have 10 career playoff game-winning goals, already a franchise record.

The narrative is cyclical, of course, as the Blackhawks of 30 years ago can attest. They were loaded with Denis Savard, Steve Larmer, Doug Wilson, Bob Murray, Al Secord and Troy Murray, among others. All of them had reason to believe they comprised at worst the second-best team in hockey. Problem: timing. They were up against the Edmonton Oilers and Wayne Gretzky.

"At any particular time, they could put six future Hall of Famers on the ice," recalled Troy Murray, currently the team's radio analyst and a foe Gretzky cited as one of his

OPPOSITE TOP: Corey Crawford gives the Soldier Field fans what they want, reprising his infamous 2013 rally speech.
OPPOSITE BOTTOM: "I've never been more proud of a team," Head Coach Joel Quenneville tells the assembled masses.

"IT'S THE COOLEST TROPHY IN SPORTS," TVR SAID. "IT MEANS SO MUCH TO AMERICANS, CANADIANS, EUROPEANS—ANYBODY WHO PLAYS HOCKEY— BECAUSE HOCKEY IS THE ULTIMATE TEAM SPORT."

most efficient shadows. "You thought you were getting close to the Oilers, and then they would kick it into another gear. If you're any of the other really good teams in our division—St. Louis, Nashville, Minnesota—or in any other division in the league building toward a Cup, I'm thinking those guys have to feel a little bit like we felt in the '80s when Edmonton was dominating."

Before them, there was Bobby Hull. He was a kid when the Blackhawks won a Stanley Cup in 1961. He imagined that would be the first of many. But it wasn't to be, and nobody admires this team more than the Hall of Fame ambassador, a United Center regular on game nights.

"I am really impressed by these kids," said Hull, who was accorded a royal Soldier Field salute. "I look at that Anaheim series. Tough games against a tough team. The Ducks tried to be physical—and they were, hitting our guys whenever they could. They thought they could wear us out. But at the end of that series, tell me, who looked tired? Who looked ready to move on? Who did move on and win it all?"

For pure appreciation of that day, this tale, Darling had to be the leader in the clubhouse. The Marco Polo of goalies, Darling played in a dozen different venues with teams that might not be found on the map, let alone Googled. Yet he and his suitcase found a home with the Blackhawks, to whom he became attached when he lived briefly in Lemont, Ill.

"I was there from second to seventh grade, the longest I stayed in one place growing up with my dad in the military," said Darling, who finished the regular season with a 1.94 goals-against average and excelled as a backup in the playoffs. "I became a big fan, especially of Eddie Belfour.

I went to games only dreaming of this. About a year ago, I signed a free-agent contract with the Blackhawks. That was the greatest day in my life. My family was in the streets for the parade the last time, in 2013, and now they're on the double-decker bus with me. To see it come full circle for me, it's just unbelievable.

"Second chances are hard to find. I made a lot of stops along the way and never gave up because I love hockey. I was fortunate, the way my career was going, ups and downs. And then I wind up in a room of superstars with the Blackhawks, who made me feel welcome from the first day. Starting right with Corey Crawford, our No. 1 and one of the best goalies in the world. He supported me, became my friend, invited me over to his house for dinner. I couldn't have asked for more.

"Then just being part of the playoffs, feeling like I belonged, trying to contribute even a little bit. Then after a two-month grind, watching how the team won and how the guys handled winning. I learned so much being around these guys. Amazing. Amazing things keep happening to me."

Michal Rozsival, a missing link on the blue line, abandoned his crutches for his appointment with the Cup. Then, before a group rendition of "We Are the Champions" and one more blast of "Chelsea Dagger," Versteeg and Joakim Nordstrom performed a brief rap intended to encourage dance. Asked what we geriatrics are supposed to call that, Nordstrom said, "I'll get back to you."

Confetti engulfed players as they exited, beaming. Did we hear that correctly? Did Teuvo Teravainen, all of 20 years old, really say he waited his whole life for this? ▓

OPPOSITE TOP: "And we laughed and had a really really really good time!" Joakim Nordstrom and Kris Versteeg entertain the crowd with an a cappella performance.

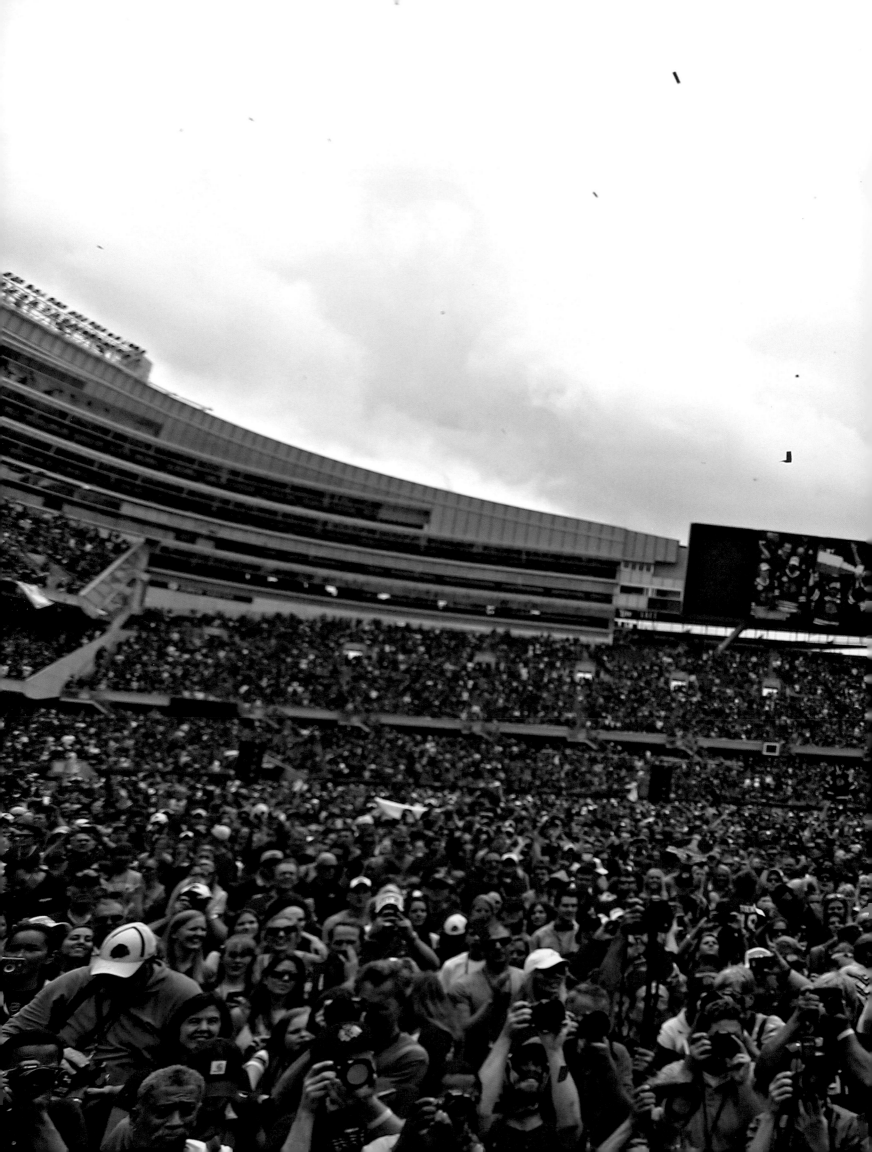

HONORING OUR FRIEND

by TROY MURRAY AND PAT FOLEY

as told to Eric Lear

Every game during the playoffs is a battle. The Blackhawks played four multi-overtime games during the postseason, including the longest contest in franchise history, but that was far from the toughest day of the season. That distinction is reserved for Sunday, Dec. 21, the day of a regular-season game at the United Center.

The team didn't have a morning skate prior to a 6 p.m. tilt with Toronto because of a road game in Columbus the night before, but when the team arrived for pregame meetings, they learned that they had lost a dear friend— Assistant Equipment Manager Clint Reif.

Clint was a special guy. There are a lot of special guys in that locker room, but to lose one of them suddenly like that is a shock to the system and one of the hardest things these players will have to go through in their careers.

Joel Quenneville talked to the media that day as he usually does, but this time with tears in his eyes. The emotion that Joel showed during that pregame press conference revealed how much the whole team loved Clint and how important Clint was to the Blackhawks.

Clint was in his ninth season in a role that can be underappreciated by those outside the locker room, but those inside know just how important he was. Clint and the entire equipment staff worked tirelessly to meet the requests of every single player so that they could perform at the highest level when they hit the ice. Any championship team talks about how important those people in the background are: They're a family.

I'm a big believer in the fact that the dynamic in the locker room plays a big part in whether a team is successful or not, and the Blackhawks are as tight-knit as they come. I wasn't in the locker room that day, but from everything I heard there was nothing said in the room the entire time before the game. There was just a numbness. I believe the players just understood what they had to do. They had to push the emotions aside and win for Clint.

They could have used any excuse in the world to play poorly, and quite frankly, I don't think anyone would've blamed them if they did. The Blackhawks ended up shutting out Toronto that night, 4-0, without emotion and without celebration.

As the season moved along, there were some definite highs and lows, but there was an inspiration from Clint inside that room for the rest of the year. He was always there. Clint was a driving force to keep things in perspective and gave the team a source of motivation.

When the Blackhawks did win it all, it was for Clint.

His presence was felt at the Soldier Field rally when Kris Versteeg stepped up to the microphone to award the championship belt for the final time. He acknowledged Patrick Kane's two-point performance in Game 6, but rather than pass it to No. 88, he handed it off to Clint's son, C.J., which I think was a tremendous gesture. Even though he's no longer with us, Clint will continue to be a big part of people's lives and inspire the team to become better people.

If you need more than that to understand how important Clint Reif was to the Blackhawks, just look at the "CR" tattooed on the right arm of Scott Darling.

— *Troy Murray, Blackhawks Radio Color Analyst*

We all struggle to find the right words in moments of sadness, even those of us who talk for a living.

I'll never forget what Jonathan Toews said on a very difficult day for all of us within the Blackhawks organization. The captain stood up in front of dozens of reporters and cameras and said that Clint Reif was so important to the Blackhawks, he might as well have been wearing a uniform. That's not something Jonathan would say lightly, and it explains profoundly what Clint meant to the team.

Out of everyone we travel with throughout the season, Clint was my favorite guy. He was a live wire. He had a lot of energy and was always positive. I don't think I ever saw

him have a bad day or a down day. I'm sure there had to be those times where something was eating at him, but he never showed it, or at least not when I was around him. He was so full of life, and that's the most shocking part about all of this.

Just as Toews did, I had to search for the right words. I thought a lot about what to say at the start of the broadcast that night because I wanted to do it properly and honor my friend. I don't remember exactly what I said, but I do remember struggling to get through it. Eddie Olczyk and I both had a hard time. It was a brutal day. To have a stunning thing happen the way it did and at the time that it did, it's hard to wrap your head around. With that said, we had a job to do, and I think we did it well given the situation.

The players had the toughest job of all. Clint was a huge part of making that locker room a special place, a place where those players wanted to be, and all of a sudden he was gone. Duncan Keith, who said he lost his best friend, might have taken it the hardest. There's no doubt in my mind that Keith took his game to another level in the second half of the season—and especially in the playoffs—because of Clint's passing. A big part of his motivation was to not leave any stone unturned for his friend. He had Clint on his mind and in his heart, and he was determined to do everything he could to win the Stanley Cup for him. A lot of us felt that way. Clint had an endearing quality about him. If you were around him, it was hard not to like him or, honestly, love him.

We all tried to express our feelings in different ways after losing our friend, but the truth is that there are no words to describe just how much of an impact he made on all of our lives.

— *Pat Foley, Blackhawks TV Play-by-Play Announcer*

A TROPHY LIKE NO OTHER

by ADAM KEMPENAAR

After three championships in six seasons, you could hardly begrudge the Blackhawks for beginning to regard the Stanley Cup as a relative—perhaps that favorite aunt or uncle who regularly drops in, bearing expensive gifts. Lord Stanley's renowned chalice may not be able to reciprocate those feelings, but its beloved protectors can.

"Here we are for the third time with the Blackhawks," said Hockey Hall of Fame Vice President and Curator Phil Pritchard. "Three great summers with the same Cup keepers each time—we like to think of ourselves as part of the family now. Hopefully the guys can do it again. If they do, we'll gladly be there."

Pritchard and his merry band of globetrotting guardians offered an oral history of the travels, tradition and transcendence of the greatest trophy in sports.

Phil Pritchard: My first Cup trip was 1988. I had gone to school and interned with the Ontario Hockey League and Canadian Hockey League, and then I got recommended for the Hockey Hall of Fame. My first or second day on the job, our boss said, "The Stanley Cup needs to go to a charity event north of Toronto. Does anyone want to go?" And nobody's volunteering, so I kind of put my hand up.

We actually did the first player day with the Cup in 1989. Colin Patterson, Calgary Flames. That, too, was kind of a fluke, and like a lot of things in hockey, it just evolved into a little tradition. So what Colin Patterson started in '89 has become a tradition for every team and every player since '95.

The 1995 New Jersey Devils were the first group of champions who got a day with the Cup, per a mandate from recently appointed National Hockey League Commissioner Gary Bettman and the trustees of the Hockey Hall of Fame. Bettman and the league recognized what the Stanley Cup meant to not just the players, "but families, friends, fans, all of that," says Pritchard.

Walt Neubrand: I graduated with a teaching degree but couldn't find a job, so in 1995 I started at the Hall of Fame, working the rink zone and tickets, stuff like that. After a couple years, Phil asked me if I wanted to be a keeper. "You start this weekend. You're going to Scotty Bowman's house."

Bowman, currently the Blackhawks' senior advisor to hockey operations, was celebrating his seventh Stanley Cup as a head coach and the first of three he would win with the Detroit Red Wings.

Mike Bolt: I was able to do Scotty Bowman's 2002 Cup day, and it never gets old, spending time with a legend like him. He's as big a fan of the game as anyone out there. He's got such an amazing collection of memorabilia and artifacts that going into his basement might be one of the coolest tours outside of the Hockey Hall of Fame.

Neubrand: I was being so careful to not go over the speed limit on the expressway [from Toronto to Bowman's home in Buffalo] because I didn't want to crash and ruin the Cup! I'm just sitting there thinking, "I'm on my way to Scotty Bowman's house. Only the winningest coach in NHL history." And we're still taking it to him. That's the funny part.

It was an easy day. He just had it in his backyard and people came and looked, and then we took it out for a ride in his old car. I was done by like 7 p.m. "Well, that was a piece of cake," I thought. Little did I know how long and involved these days would get.

Bill Wellman: I think most guys will tell you that planning your Cup day is worse than planning your wedding. They always say the second time around is so much better because the first is just a blur of activities that you barely remember. The second isn't necessarily scaled back, but you're a little bit more relaxed knowing that everything is going to go fine. This third time for some Blackhawks—that's a rare luxury. They get to learn from their past experiences and change it up.

Howie Borrow: Everybody wants a piece of it, and

OPPOSITE: Duncan Keith shows off the Stanley Cup to fans at Wrigley Field the day after Game 6.

the players always do their best. Local rinks where they might've played as a kid, children's hospitals, police and fire stations. Even after three times in six years, it doesn't get old. They still want to celebrate with everybody.

Bolt: It's all about the community and family. Rarely do the players just get to sit back and enjoy the Stanley Cup. For a guy on his third, you really could make it all about you. But the Blackhawks were still able to share it, in their hometowns or wherever they happened to be.

Pritchard: They get the team atmosphere; they know it's not just about them. At the same time, it's always nice when it's a quiet event and they're just with their families and friends, or their moms and dads, and they're looking at the Cup names. They've got that sense of accomplishment and can share it with the ones they love.

Bolt: I told the guys back in 2010, "Make sure you find time for yourself and a small group of your friends and family. Have the Cup on a table and enjoy the history of it, really let it sink in that you're a Stanley Cup champion and your name is going alongside some of the great names, from Bobby Hull and Stan Mikita to Ted Lindsay, Wayne Gretzky and Mario Lemieux." Guys were always appreciative when I mentioned that, because sometimes with their first Stanley Cup they don't think to do it.

Pritchard: Whenever a Final ends, you know that the best team has won. And you certainly understand how and why the Blackhawks are the best when you hang out with them during the summer. Obviously, with the first of the three Cups they were a younger team, and you could see how Joel Quenneville and the coaches and Rocky Wirtz and John McDonough and everybody in the front office brought the group together as a family. This year when they won it, you could see them all maturing, not only as a family, but as a unit and a team.

I think the fans also grew as a family and a team. Chicago sports fans are unbelievable. I don't even know what to say about them. Their passion is phenomenal, and to see it at every event in Chicago—and around the world—is pretty incredible.

Borrow: We get to travel everywhere. I spent 12 days in Europe this summer. Different cultures, but the fans still celebrate like they do here.

Neubrand: I had been to Finland before, but it was a thrill for me to take it to a veteran guy like Kimmo

Timonen. I've followed him his whole career. You could just see it in his face, how excited he was. Sixteen seasons culminated in that moment. And then there's a rookie like Teuvo Teravainen, who took it to Sauna Island in Helsinki. That was interesting, just an island full of saunas where he and his friends got to relax.

Pritchard: It's always special to see what the European guys have done, how they've brought this market, this team, to their individual countries and hometowns. The number of Blackhawks jerseys we saw at Timonen's day was unbelievable.

Wellman: Cruising down the Vltava River in Prague with Michal Rozsival was incredible.

Bolt: We went out in a boat with Jonathan Toews up in Lake of the Woods in Ontario. He and his buddies had the Cup in the boat, and he's out wakeboarding and taking pictures—it was an absolutely beautiful day. You'd have to ask Jonathan, but I know he was just really taking it all in and enjoying the fact that the Stanley Cup was sitting in his own backyard again.

Neubrand: I had the Cup with Brad Richards in 2004 when he won with Tampa Bay. He was a little wilder then. Now he's got a son, and it was nice to see his family again. Going to Prince Edward Island is always really cool. It's a very rural, kind of laid-back atmosphere.

Borrow: I had a lot of fun with Brent Seabrook going out to Vancouver. He picked us up in helicopters. We did some flying around, went up to the top of a mountain area

OPPOSITE TOP: Hockey Hall of Fame Cup Keepers Phil Pritchard, Bill Wellman, Howie Borrow and Mike Bolt pose with the Conn Smythe Trophy, Stanley Cup, Clarence Campbell Bowl and William M. Jennings Trophy at the United Center.
OPPOSITE BOTTOM: Jonathan Toews wakeboards behind a boat carrying the Stanley Cup.
ABOVE: Teuvo Teravainen looks on as Kimmo Timonen hoists the Stanley Cup before thousands of fans in his hometown in Finland.

ABOVE: Brent Seabrook and son, Carter, bond with the Stanley Cup atop a mountain in British Columbia.
OPPOSITE TOP: Lemont, Ill., native Scott Darling begins his Cup day with a ride on a retro Lemont Fire Department truck.
OPPOSITE BOTTOM: Towing the Stanley Cup, Niklas Hjalmarsson leads a group in his home village of Russnäs, Sweden.

ABOVE TOP: Teuvo Teravainen raises the Cup in Helsinki.
ABOVE BOTTOM: Patrick Sharp and daughter Madelyn take the Cup out near the water in Niantic, Conn.
OPPOSITE TOP: Duncan Keith shares the Cup with a patient at La Verendrye General Hospital in Fort Frances, Ontario.
OPPOSITE BOTTOM: Kimmo Timonen enjoys another Cup hoist in Kuopio, Finland.

and got some nice footage. Brent wanted some memorable moments with the Cup and his family that he could cherish for the rest of his life, and he got them.

Neubrand: Antoine Vermette was the same in the first minute of the day as he was in the last minute when he took it to the public [in his hometown of Saint-Agapit, Quebec]. He made sure everybody got pictures; he was very caring. You often see guys kind of wearing down, but he kept going.

Wellman: When we were in Trenčín, Slovakia, with Marian Hossa at that castle that dates back to 180 A.D., that blew my socks off. That was the tip of the Roman Empire. I mean, what the heck is a guy like me doing there? The Cup has given me the opportunity to see and do more than I ever would have otherwise.

Pritchard: There is some magic to it. What sets the Cup apart from all the other championship trophies is the aura and tradition of it. People often don't appreciate what it is until they see it in person. Then you tell them the first year a team won it was 1893, and it really sinks in. When you're with a player and he's looking at where his name is going to go, and you see him find a guy he grew up idolizing, that stuff is so powerful and emotional. The emotion is the thing that makes the Cup what it is. You try to talk to some of the players, and they're speechless when they win it.

Bolt: I remember years ago I had it up at Safeco Field where the Seattle Mariners play. We were doing a promo

for national TV, and the Mariners and Red Sox players were coming over to the Cup. One guy says, "You know the Stanley Cup is so cool, they get their names on it." Another ballplayer goes, "They get to take it home for a day." Another goes, "They get to drink out of it, eat out of it." And another goes, "We play for a bunch of stinking flags." I thought it was pretty funny.

Neubrand: Take the World Series trophy or a Super Bowl trophy. It's new. No one has really touched it, no one has done anything with it. It doesn't have a history. But the Stanley Cup has been around for 123 years, and it's the same one that Gretzky, Lemieux, Steve Yzerman…

Borrow: …Maurice Richard, Gordie Howe and Bobby Orr…

Neubrand: …Every one of them has had time with it. And now it's your time. Even if you're standing up there for 10 seconds after waiting in a line for three hours, you are with that Cup, the same one. All of the teams that have won those other trophies have got one, but nobody owns the Stanley Cup.

Wellman: It's just the coolest thing ever. As a kid, whenever we'd go to my grandparents' house, I'd bug my mom and dad to drop me off at the Hockey Hall of Fame at the Canadian National Exhibition Grounds. I would literally run in and look at the 1972 Team Canada display and a few other exhibits. Then the highlight, the Stanley Cup. After that, I'd run back out to the car and we'd drive on. I often think back to that, and even today when I open the Cup case, it's a pretty special feeling.

Bolt: I watched the Stanley Cup finals as a kid, too. You see your favorite players raise it on the ice, and for these guys to be able to do the same thing that some of their idols have done, that's what makes it so emotional. Every hockey player dreams about getting his name on the Stanley Cup.

Borrow: So much hard work that has gone into it over the years. When the players finally get to raise it, that's the moment. You've finally reached that ultimate goal.

Wellman: It doesn't matter who wins it, I get that little tingly feeling through my body whenever I watch the captain hoist the Cup. Just that absolute exhilaration. The little asterisk for me is that I'm the last one to really give it a good polishing. I'm thrilled to see it glisten as it goes out onto the ice. ▥

ABOVE: Sadie and Madelyn Sharp embrace the Cup.
OPPOSITE TOP: Trenčín Castle in Marian Hossa's hometown in Slovakia is all decked out for Hossa's arrival with the Stanley Cup.
OPPOSITE BOTTOM: Michal Rozsival takes the Cup on a boat tour down the Vltava River in Prague.

OPPOSITE AND ABOVE: (Clockwise) Marian Hossa, Assistant General Manager Norm Maciver, Antoine Vermette, Brad Richards, Brent Seabrook and Niklas Hjalmarsson enjoy some special time with the Stanley Cup.

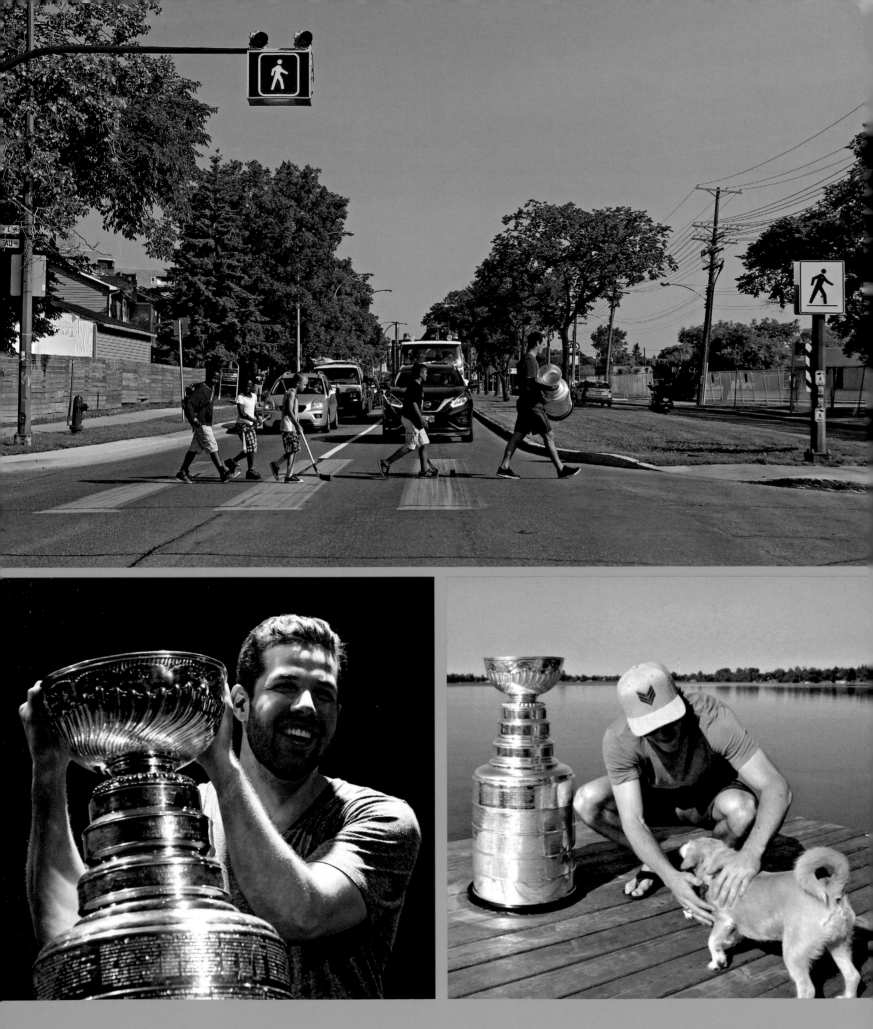

ABOVE TOP: Jonathan Toews crosses a street with the Cup in Winnipeg as local kids trail behind.
ABOVE BOTTOM LEFT: Corey Crawford basks in the Cup's glow during his day in Châteauguay, Quebec.
ABOVE BOTTOM RIGHT: Andrew Shaw plays with his dog Bailey by a lake in Belleville, Ontario.
OPPOSITE: Assistant Coach Kevin Dineen, Michal Rozsival, Shaw and Head Coach Joel Quenneville present the Stanley Cup to fans at U.S. Cellular Field on June 21.

WINNING MEANS SHARING

by BOB VERDI

On a steamy day last August, summer campers at the Center for Independence through Conductive Education were asked to ponder the future. With youngsters challenged by physical disabilities, such an endeavor provides motivation. What are your plans for college? Do you want to further your education in a certain area? Is there a particular occupation that interests you?

"Understand that these are people learning to do things that most of us take for granted," said Patti Herbst, executive director of the non-profit project. "Walking, sitting, eating, toileting. Part of our program is job training, vocational skills. Looking ahead, thinking ahead, achieving independence. Well, that day our topic went off on a little tangent when a girl named Sophia, a huge hockey fan, suddenly brought up the Blackhawks."

Sophia Jablonski, a driven 16-year-old with cerebral palsy, essentially produced and directed a video so she and her classmates could congratulate their favorite team on a third Stanley Cup in six years. And oh, by the way, wouldn't it be great if they could see the Cup in person?

"About a month later, just after Labor Day, we started

school in Countryside, one of our three locations in the Chicago area," Herbst continued. "We told the children we were going to celebrate with two special guests. In walked Andrew Shaw with the Stanley Cup! There must have been 60 kids in the classroom, and they just couldn't believe it! Lots of ear-to-ear smiles.

"And let me tell you about Andrew Shaw. Right away he understood. He told them that he too had to train—obviously on a different level—to become what he wanted to be, a great hockey player. He did not leave until he talked to every one of our kids. The idea of all this was to congratulate the Blackhawks. Andrew Shaw wound up congratulating them. Wonderful. Just wonderful."

Such is the magic spread by the Stanley Cup. At 35 or so pounds, it is the undisputed heavyweight champion of sports trophies in North America, if not around the world. With the globalization of the National Hockey League, this shiny silver beauty has entranced even casual fans, time and again, on multiple continents. Indeed, the Cup gets older, yet seeing it never gets old.

"Fortunately, 'the Cup' has become part of Chicago's vernacular," said Blackhawks President and CEO John McDonough. "It doesn't need to be qualified by saying 'The Stanley Cup.' It has so much history. It's so real. It's got a few dents in it. And of course it's not only a lifetime memory to have your picture taken with it—the Cup is a great fundraiser for charitable causes."

Other sports trophies are won, hailed, then hidden in glass cases. But only hours after the Blackhawks eliminated the Tampa Bay Lightning in Game 6 of the Final on June 15, the Stanley Cup went public to a landscape with which it has become quite familiar—the streets of Chicago. To be touched, to be photographed, to be savored. In no sport does the ultimate prize keep such hours or log so many miles.

What's better is that although it can go it alone, the Stanley Cup invariably appears with a player or players or members of the organization who helped make a

OPPOSITE: The Stanley Cup rides on WGN Radio's float in the 46th Annual Chicago Pride Parade on June 28.

DEAR MR. MC DONOUGH:
THANKS FOR BRINGING THE STANLEY CUP TO LEO H.S.

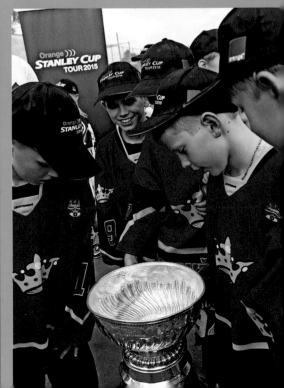

"WITH THE CUP, WE CAN HELP WHERE HELP IS NEEDED AND BE BETTER AT FULFILLING OUR RESPONSIBILITY," MCDONOUGH SAID. "FANS DON'T ALWAYS SEE PICTURES OF WHERE IT GOES FOR MOST OF THE SUMMER, PLACES WHERE IT MEANS SO MUCH."

championship possible. And what's best of all is that the Stanley Cup seems to have a soul, a spirit.

"I've always said the Cup is at its best when it is creating a distraction or providing a few moments of enjoyment for those who really need it," said Jay Blunk, the Blackhawks' executive vice president. "It brings a focus to a cause or a certain situation that might otherwise have been overlooked. Taking the Cup to our fans is as important as anything we do."

Blunk took the Cup to Danvers, Ill. Citizens there used the occasion as a fundraiser for Delavan, an adjacent town devastated by a tornado in mid-July. Chairman Rocky Wirtz took the Cup to a firehouse near his home. At Leo High School on Chicago's South Side, students thought it would be just another day until McDonough and Brent Seabrook showed up with the Cup. Then Blunk got it again to present it at a benefit for the USO of Illinois, with which the Blackhawks have formed a bond.

"People just can't get enough of it," McDonough said. "With the Cup, we can help where help is needed and be better at fulfilling our responsibility. Fans see newspaper pictures of it from the night our team clinched, but they don't always see pictures of where it goes for most of the summer, places where it means so much."

Vice President/General Manager Stan Bowman again accompanied the Cup he was named after to the University of Chicago Medical Center. He also did it in 2013. Five years earlier, he was a patient there fighting cancer. Head Coach Joel Quenneville, a Chicagoland resident year-round, had the Cup at a hospital near his home. Captain Jonathan Toews, who hails from Winnipeg, carried the Cup to a local community center bearing his name, then to the Rehabilitation Centre for Children.

Duncan Keith and the Cup went to a hospital in Ontario, Goaltending Coach Jimmy Waite to a hospital in Quebec, David Rundblad to a school in Sweden, Bryan Bickell to The Hospital for Sick Children in Toronto, Marian Hossa to a hospital in Slovakia, and the same with Michal Rozsival in the Czech Republic. After all the hours he puts in to keep the Blackhawks healthy, Head Athletic Trainer Mike Gapski could have planted the Cup in his backyard and admired it from a hammock. Instead he put the Cup to work, gathering support for the Special Olympics and Big Brothers Big Sisters.

"I'm proud of how our players and our staff respond on their days with the Cup," McDonough concluded. "That's the thing. It's only one day that they have it. It's not one week. But the people in this organization have their priorities in the right place. The Blackhawks are part of the community and part of communities all over the world."

Indeed, the Blackhawks are quite experienced and rather adept at the regimen involving their dear friend, the Stanley Cup.

Win it. Enjoy it. Share it. ◫

2015 STANLEY CUP TRACKER

by **SEAN GRADY**

1 **CHICAGO CUBS** vs **CLEVELAND INDIANS**
June 16, 2015 • Wrigley Field, Chicago, IL, USA

2 **STANLEY CUP RALLY & PARADE**
June 18, 2015 • Soldier Field, Chicago, IL, USA

3 **CHICAGO WHITE SOX** vs **TEXAS RANGERS**
June 21, 2015 • U.S. Cellular Field, Chicago, IL, USA

4 **SCOTT DARLING'S CUP DAY**
June 29, 2015 • Lemont, IL, USA

5 **BRYAN BICKELL'S CUP DAY**
July 2, 2015 • Toronto, ON, CAN

6 **ANDREW SHAW'S CUP DAY**
July 4, 2015 • Belleville, ON, CAN

7 **ANDREW DESJARDINS' CUP DAY**
July 6, 2015 • Sudbury, ON, CAN

8 **MIKE KITCHEN'S CUP DAY**
July 8, 2015 • Aurora, ON, CAN

9 **JONATHAN TOEWS' CUP DAY**
July 10, 2015 • Winnipeg, MB, CAN

10 **COREY CRAWFORD'S CUP DAY**
July 12, 2015 • Montreal, QC, CAN

11 **JIMMY WAITE'S CUP DAY**
July 13, 2015 • Sherbrooke, QC, CAN

12 **TROY PARCHMAN'S CUP DAY**
July 15, 2015 • Chicago, IL, USA

13 **TONY OMMEN'S CUP DAY**
July 16, 2015 • Bolingbrook, IL, USA

14 **BLACKHAWKS CONVENTION**
July 17-18, 2015 • Hilton Hotel, Chicago, IL, USA

15 **TEUVO TERAVAINEN'S CUP DAY**
July 20, 2015 • Helsinki, FIN

16 **KIMMO TIMONEN'S CUP DAY**
July 22, 2015 • Kuopio, FIN

17 **ANTTI RAANTA'S CUP DAY**
July 23, 2015 • Rauma, FIN

18 **ANTOINE VERMETTE'S CUP DAY**
July 25, 2015 • Quebec City, QC, CAN

19 **PATRICK SHARP'S CUP DAY**
July 26, 2015 • Niantic, CT, USA

20 **BRAD RICHARDS' CUP DAY**
July 27, 2015 • Murray Harbour, PEI, CAN

21 **BRANDON SAAD'S CUP DAY**
July 29, 2015 • Pittsburgh, PA, USA

22 **TREVOR VAN RIEMSDYK'S CUP DAY**
July 30, 2015 • Middletown, NJ, USA

23 **DUNCAN KEITH'S CUP DAY**
August 1, 2015 • Fort Frances, ON, CAN

24 **KRIS VERSTEEG'S CUP DAY**
August 2, 2015 • Lethbridge, ON, CAN

25 **KYLE CUMISKEY'S CUP DAY**
August 3, 2015 • Abbotsford, BC, CAN

26 **PAWEL PRYLINSKI'S CUP DAY**
August 5, 2015 • Chicago, IL, USA

27 **JOEL QUENNEVILLE'S CUP DAY**
August 6, 2015 • Chicago, IL, USA

28 **SCOTTY BOWMAN'S CUP DAY**
August 7, 2015 • Buffalo, NY, USA

29 **PATRICK KANE'S CUP DAY**
August 8, 2015 • Buffalo, NY, USA

30 **ROCKY WIRTZ'S CUP DAY**
August 9, 2015 • Wilmette, IL, USA

31 **KEVIN DINEEN'S CUP DAY**
August 10, 2015 • Queensbury, NY, USA

32 **MATT MEACHAM'S CUP DAY**
August 11, 2015 • Massena, NY, USA

33 **NORM MACIVER'S CUP DAY**
August 12, 2015 • Duluth, MN, USA

34 **MIKE GAPSKI'S CUP DAY**
August 13, 2015 • Chicago, IL, USA

35 **BRENT SEABROOK'S CUP DAY**
August 16, 2015 • Kelowna, BC, CAN

36 **JOHNNY ODUYA & MARCUS KRUGER'S CUP DAY**
August 18, 2015 • Stockholm, SWE

37 **JOAKIM NORDSTROM'S CUP DAY**
August 19, 2015 • Stockholm, SWE

38 **MARIAN HOSSA'S CUP DAY**
August 21, 2015 • Trenčín, SVK

39 **MICHAL ROZSIVAL'S CUP DAY**
August 22, 2015 • Prague, CZE

40 **NIKLAS HJALMARSSON'S CUP DAY**
August 25, 2015 • Russnäs, SWE

41 **DAVID RUNDBLAD'S CUP DAY**
August 27, 2015 • Skellefteå, SWE

42 **JOHN MCDONOUGH'S CUP DAY**
August 29, 2015 • Edison Park, Chicago, IL, USA

43 **DANIEL CARCILLO'S CUP DAY**
August 30, 2015 • Chicago, IL, USA

44 **JEFF THOMAS' CUP DAY**
September 1, 2015 • Chicago, IL, USA

45 **AL MACISAAC'S CUP DAY**
September 2, 2015 • Antigonish, NS, CAN

46 **DR. MICHAEL TERRY'S CUP DAY**
September 3, 2015 • Chicago, IL, USA

47 **PAUL GOODMAN'S CUP DAY**
September 4, 2015 • Saugatuck, MI, USA

48 **JIM HEINTZELMAN'S CUP DAY**
September 6, 2015 • Grand Rapids, MI, USA

49 **STAN BOWMAN'S CUP DAY**
September 11, 2015 • Chicago, IL, USA

50 **NORTHWESTERN** vs **EASTERN ILLINOIS**
September 12, 2015 • Ryan Field, Evanston, IL, USA

51 **JAY BLUNK'S CUP DAY**
September 13, 2015 • Wilmette, IL, USA

52 **TRAINING CAMP AT NOTRE DAME**
September 18-20, 2015 • South Bend, IN, USA

53 **CHICAGO BEARS** vs **OAKLAND RAIDERS**
October 4, 2015 • Soldier Field, Chicago, IL, USA

54 **BANNER RAISING CEREMONY**
October 7, 2015 • United Center, Chicago, IL, USA

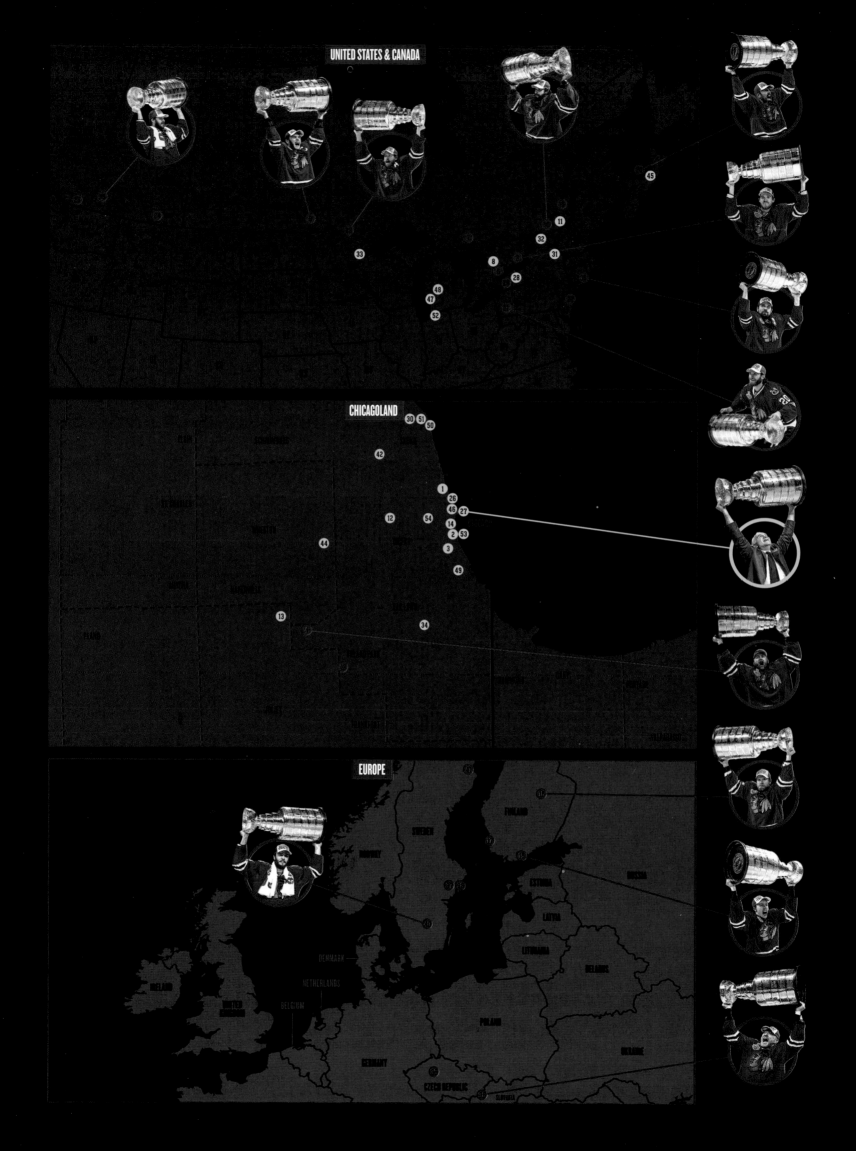

UNITED STATES & CANADA

CHICAGOLAND

EUROPE

GREG DE VRIES CHRISTIAN NANCHRIS DRURY ADAM FOOTE
PETER FORSBERG MILAN HEJDUK DAN HINOTE
JON KLEMM ERIC MESSIER BRYAN MUIR VILLE NIEMINEN
SCOTT PARKER SHJON PODEIN NOLAN PRATT DAVID REID
STEVEN REINPRECHT PATRICK ROY JOE SAKIC
MARTIN SKOULA ALEX TANGUAY STEPHANE YELLE

STEVE YZERMAN
MATHIEU DAN
NICKLAS L
BOYD DEVER
BRETT H
LUC ROBIT

CHICAGO BLACKHAWKS 2014-15

W. ROCKWELL WIRTZ JOHN McDONOUGH JAY BLUNK
STAN BOWMAN AL MACISAAC NORM MACIVER SCOTTY BOWMAN
JOEL QUENNEVILLE MIKE KITCHEN KEVIN DINEEN
JIMMY WAITE MIKE GAPSKI TROY PARCHMAN JEFF THOMAS
PAWEL PRYLINSKI JIM HEINTZELMAN PAUL GOODMAN
MATT MEACHAM PIERRE GAUTHIER MARK KELLEY
BARRY SMITH RYAN STEWART RON ANDERSON
TONY OMMEN MARK BERNARD DR. MICHAEL TERRY
JONATHAN TOEWS CAPT. PATRICK KANE MARIAN HOSSA BRANDON SAAD
DUNCAN KEITH PATRICK SHARP BRAD RICHARDS KRIS VERSTEEG
BRENT SEABROOK BRYAN BICKELL ANDREW SHAW NIKLAS HJALMARSSON
MARCUS KRUGER DAVID RUNDBLAD MICHAL ROZSIVAL JOHNNY ODUYA
TEUVO TERAVAINEN ANTOINE VERMETTE ANDREW DESJARDINS
TREVOR VAN RIEMSDYK KIMMO TIMONEN KYLE CUMISKEY
COREY CRAWFORD SCOTT DARLING DANIEL CARCILLO JOAKIM NORDSTROM

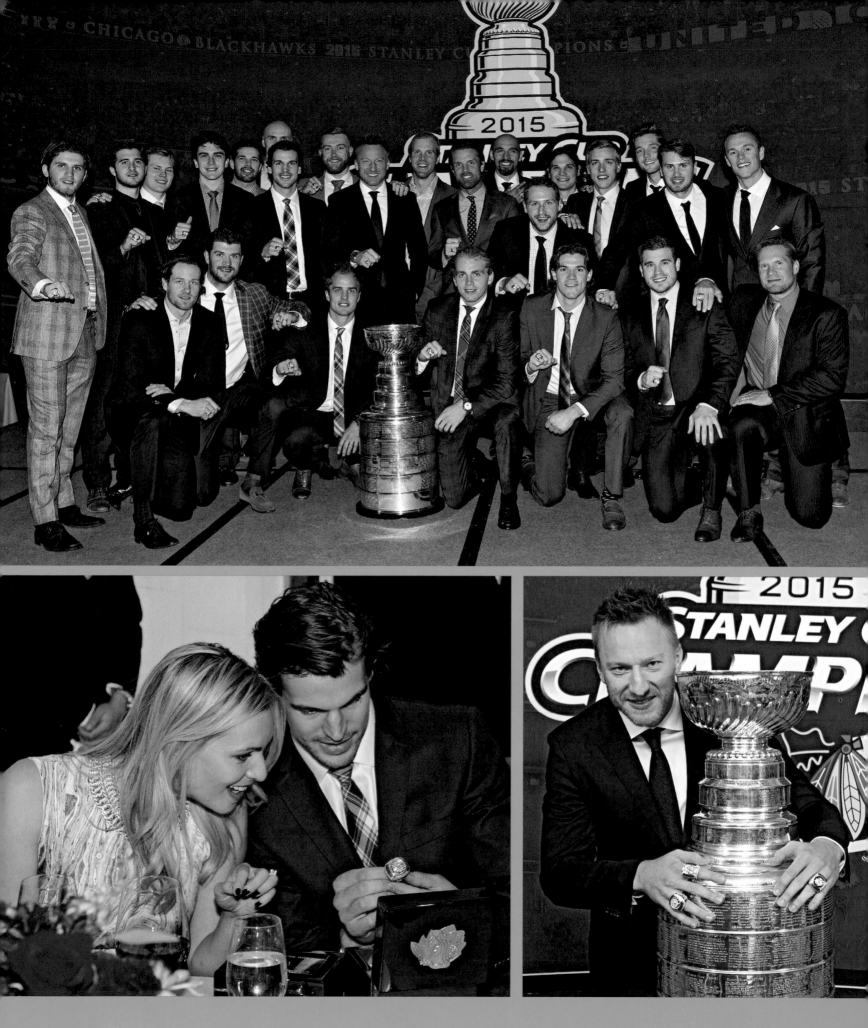

ABOVE TOP: Members of the 2015 championship team pose with their new hardware at the ring ceremony on Oct. 4, 2015.
ABOVE BOTTOM LEFT: Antoine Vermette and his wife, Karen, examine the ring.
ABOVE BOTTOM RIGHT: Marian Hossa hugs the Cup while wearing all three of his championship rings.

GETTING CROWDED UP THERE

by BOB VERDI

Until recently, finding a place for championship laundry hasn't exactly been a pressing issue for the Blackhawks. But suddenly, it's getting a bit crowded up there in the United Center rafters.

On opening night, Oct. 7, hockey's best team celebrated its third Stanley Cup in six seasons by raising the 2015 banner to the ceiling. As white as the ice below, the newest flag secured a spot in a marvelously tight fit between keepsakes from 2010 and 2013.

Once upon a time, the pennant collection seemed tilted toward the building's west side, freighted by a half-dozen honoring the Bulls, who earned theirs with a pair of three-peats produced and directed by Michael Jordan.

But now, with this distinguished group of Blackhawks, the interior decorating at the facility has been altered. The United Center's cotenants on skates also own six, although the spacing of titles is pure staccato compared with the rhythmic display of the banners themselves.

From 1926, when the franchise was born, to 1961—three. Pause. From 2010 to 2015—three, thanks mightily to a core group of players who stared at the most rigid

financial system in professional sports and left it in their rearview mirrors.

Such symmetry, albeit delayed, is fun. So are xylobands. Those are LED wristbands synchronized to throbbing music and spectacular videos, both of which were in abundance for a ceremony that could have commanded a standalone admittance fee. (Not that the 2015-16 season's first Blackhawks goal, scored by Russian waterbug Artemi Panarin, or the second by another prodigy, Teuvo Teravainen, was too much for 22,104 fans to handle.)

Every soul inside the arena was riveted, save for the visiting New York Rangers, who tuned it all out in their quarters. It isn't everywhere that adult males in dark suits elicit ear-splitting ovations, but this is Chicago, where hockey fever has reached epidemic levels after a protracted remission.

For decades the Stanley Cup was a rumor around here, except when opponents lifted it across the street at the grand old Stadium. Some years the Blackhawks were better at golf than hockey. A healthy scratch was a guy who could really play…the wrong sport. The media watched games so you didn't have to. Simply put, the Blackhawks were irrelevant in 2007 when Chairman Rocky Wirtz and President and CEO John McDonough arrived as first responders on the accident scene.

For organizing the organization, and for engineering a resurrection so rapidly, they were hailed on opening night, loud and long. Also introduced by TV Color Analyst Eddie Olczyk were two other brains behind the brawn: Vice President/General Manager Stan Bowman and Head Coach Joel Quenneville. Another rolling thunderclap of applause.

"I think that was the fans' way of thanking people who helped bring hockey back here," noticed Trevor Daley after his first game with the Blackhawks. "I played here with Dallas when the arena was half-empty. Pretty quiet after the national anthem.

"But now, even on hot days, people all over the city

THE CAP HAS DONE ITS JOB, BUT NO BETTER THAN THE BLACKHAWKS HAVE DONE THEIRS.

wear Blackhawks gear. It's quite a connection between the fans and the team. When I was traded here, I got a call from Richie (Brad Richards). I played with him on the Stars. He was here last year. He told me what to expect. First class, all the way."

Niklas Hjalmarsson wheeled out of the Zamboni chute with the Stanley Cup and placed it on a table at center ice. One of six current Blackhawks to be fitted for three rings, Hjalmarsson glided 100 feet without blocking a single shot. Quite possibly a career first.

The Cup stayed there until Jonathan Toews came out last and hoisted it above his shoulders, an exercise that must have felt as familiar to the peerless captain as brushing his teeth. Duncan Keith soon uprooted the Cup and carried it a few yards to the east end, unofficially his shortest shift since age 3.

Everybody, players and staff, then stood for photographs while the banner came out of hiding and was unfurled for its journey straight to the rafters. Everybody included Kimmo Timonen, a grizzled defenseman who completed a splendid career with a cameo appearance last spring. He was stoked to be invited to Chicago for the dispersal of rings a couple days prior and opening night.

It was a nice touch by the Blackhawks, who are rather proficient in that department. Current events suggest they are the best team in the city, but the Blackhawks don't pack enough hubris to imagine they are the only team in the city. The Cubs were playing a significant game in Pittsburgh that same night, and their victory was part of the in-house entertainment.

Earlier that afternoon, the Blackhawks staged their annual red carpet fête along Madison Street. It was literally covered by helicopters. For a team toiling indoors, the Blackhawks have to lead the league in helicopters. But wherever these players go, it's a happening. Witness the fan festival that initiates training camp. Who or what attracts so many people to watch practice? University

of Alabama football? Blue Angels? Taylor Swift? The Blackhawks used to be enjoyed more by their foes than their fans. Not lately.

Denis Savard, the Blackhawks' Hall of Fame ambassador, warmed the crowd up. Brent Seabrook, the last man on the ice for every period, was first to emerge from Gate 3 1/2 via the spiffy new locker room. He and Keith debuted in 2005 to echoes. Now they are fathers and champions thrice over. Seabrook has donned an "A" as alternate captain—a "no-brainer," according to Quenneville. For the red carpet affair, however, the Blackhawks were in civilian clothes. No changes there. These guys not only know how to win, they know how to dress.

Toews thanked the fans, another exercise he has down cold. Ambassadors Bobby Hull and Tony Esposito were greeted royally, as was the Stanley Cup, which enjoyed a curtain call, if you will, following its appearance at the June 15 clincher. The Cup has been all over the world this summer, but still has spent so much time in Chicago that it might as well be a resident paying tax. It is a party animal, although it visits more hospitals than bars.

The hard cap instituted in 2005 was intended to foster parity and obviate the best and/or richest NHL franchises from collecting and keeping talent. The cap has done its job, but no better than the Blackhawks have done theirs.

To amass three Cups in six years would have been filed away as an absolute shocker, except that chummy gathering of six banners proves it is so. The Blackhawks have had to part with more quality players than any franchise, and they have veered toward the third rail in a few playoff series. But no team has played through forced absences and payroll restrictions with such success.

The Blackhawks aren't breaking any rules, but the rules aren't breaking the Blackhawks either.

Yes, it's getting crowded up there in the United Center rafters. But the 2015 banner looks comfortable—and amenable to moving over for more company. ▥

OPPOSITE TOP: Xylobands light up the United Center crowd prior to the banner raising.
OPPOSITE BOTTOM: Niklas Hjalmarsson has the honor of carrying the Cup out during pregame introductions.

ACKNOWLEDGMENTS

by ADAM KEMPENAAR

Crowding in the names of everyone who contributed to "One Goal III" in the space allotted here would require the precision needed to engrave the 52 representatives of each championship team on the Stanley Cup. Lacking such talent, I submit my humble etching featuring some of the individuals whose dedication and passion were essential to producing a book that we hope is worthy of the 2014-15 Chicago Blackhawks.

Thank you to **Jamie Carter**, for constantly assuring us we were still on schedule even when we most certainly were not.

Thank you to **Bob Verdi**, for your unmatched wit, eloquence and ability to elevate even the most mundane moments into the sublime.

Thank you to **Emerald Gao**, for the clarity of your writing and your obsessive consideration of every comma.

Thank you to **John Sandberg**, for your sharp eye and relentless pursuit of design perfection.

Thank you to **Stan Bowman**, **Joel Quenneville**, **Jonathan Toews** and the entire Blackhawks team, for your achievements on the ice that compelled this project, and for your accessibility off the ice that made the process of completing it so special.

Thank you to **Rocky Wirtz**, for your commitment and support that drive everything we do at 1901 West Madison Street.

Finally, thank you to **John McDonough** and **Jay Blunk**, for your continued guidance and encouragement. Through three publications over the past six seasons, your only mandate—do whatever it takes to create the best championship book possible—remains our "One Goal."

CHICAGO BLACKHAWKS 2015 STANLEY CUP CHAMPIONS

CHICAGO BLACKHAWKS 2015 STANLEY CUP CHAMPIONS

CHICAGO BLACKHAWKS 2015 STANLEY CUP CHAMPIONS